Chicago
History for Kids

Triumphs and Tragedies of the Windy City

Includes **21** Activities

Owen Hurd

CHICAGO REVIEW PRESS

Library of Congress Cataloging-in-Publication Data

Hurd, Owen.

    Chicago history for kids : triumphs and tragedies of the windy city, includes 21 activities / Owen Hurd. — 1st ed.

    p. cm.

    Includes bibliographical references and index.

    ISBN-13: 978-1-55652-654-1

    ISBN-10: 1-55652-654-7

    1. Chicago (Ill.)—History—Juvenile literature.
2. Chicago (Ill.)—History—Study and teaching—Activity programs—Juvenile literature. 3. Creative activities and seat work. 4. Chicago (Ill.)—Tours. 5. Historic sites—Illinois—Chicago—Guidebooks. I. Title.

F548.33.H87 2007
977.3'11—dc22

2006031807

www.chicagohistoryforkids.com

Cover and interior design: Joan Sommers Design

Front cover images: (clockwise from left) lion statue courtesy Jim Cole / Alamy; skyline courtesy Visions of America, LLC / Alamy; Ferris wheel courtesy North Wind Picture Archives / Alamy; "Cloud Gate" by Anish Kapoor, photo by Dan Price; 1871 ruins from Chicago fire courtesy Chicago History Museum

Back cover images: souvenir button courtesy Chicago History Museum; Adrian C. Anson courtesy Library of Congress

©2007 by Owen Hurd
First edition
Published by Chicago Review Press, Incorporated
814 North Franklin Street
Chicago, Illinois 60610
ISBN 978-1-55652-654-1
Printed in China
5 4 3 2

Contents

To Patrick and Geralyn
    For making me the luckiest man
in the history of Chicago

To Mom and Dad
    For raising five pretty good kids

To Mei Mei
    We can't wait to meet you

FOREWORD

BY CHICAGO HISTORY MUSEUM PRESIDENT GARY T. JOHNSON

CHICAGO HISTORY FOR KIDS is an exciting ride through one of the most colorful stories of any place in the world—the city of Chicago.

"Once upon a time" are four of the most exciting words in the English language, especially if they are followed by "a long, long time ago." This book begins a very long time ago, when the land that became Chicago was shaped by volcanoes, oceans, and glaciers.

This is not the usual kind of history. It ranges across conventional boundaries, so that ecology is part of the story. The Native Americans who lived in what became Chicago are not pre-history, but are history.

Kids, of course, won't notice how unusual this approach is. They just want to know what happened, and the livelier the better. They will love this book.

What makes this book special is the learning activities. Too often, the usual list of activities associated with history is short: mapmaking and dioramas and very little else. Here, many activities are more typical of science fairs than history fairs: build a miniature glacier, re-create the Chicago River watershed, make a pinhole camera. The author also uses the arts: create your own Impressionist painting, make a stained glass window, write a poem about your street. There is even a recipe for homemade caramel corn!

Kids will get their hands dirty with these activities, and they will have lots of fun— but all these activities have a point. They are offered in context and connected with a specific point in the story.

The narrative itself is quite a ride. It includes politicians and musicians, gangsters and athletes. The author's interpretation draws on a wide range of primary and secondary sources to re-create life in different periods of Chicago history, and there always is an eye to adding something special. Sidebars include topics such as a walking tour of Graceland Cemetery and an explanation of why we say "cooler near the lake."

The Great Migration from the South is here, as well as immigration from other countries. The ups and downs of Chicago sports are told—stories of pride and frustration. When the near past comes into view, readers, of course, will have their own opinions. The events surrounding the 1968 Democratic National Convention are an example.

To my mind, the best part of it all is the way that Owen Hurd reminds us of a Chicago that sometimes we can hardly imagine: "When the city was still country." But has that place vanished entirely? Of course not! The lake is still here. The river is still here. The soil is still here, and so is the weather. And the city is still here, in a place that first made sense because it was convenient for fur traders and canoes but now makes sense for international travel.

As with the best children's books, this book isn't only for children. This is a wonderful resource for parents and teachers with activities at home and around town. If they read the story and the sidebars, adults will enrich their understanding of their city.

ACKNOWLEDGMENTS

THIS BOOK WOULD NOT have been possible without the cooperation and participation of many individuals and institutions.

Joan Sommers deserves my special thanks. She was the first one to suggest that I write this book. She also did an excellent job of designing the book and its cover and made great improvements to the art project in chapter 8.

Linda Bechtle, Clare Abbene, and Douglas Knox read every page of the manuscript and made many insightful edits and suggestions. Bill Hurd provided editorial guidance on several early chapters.

Several kids read portions of the book and provided valuable feedback. My most dedicated kid editors were my son Patrick Hurd and his cousins Eamon Hurd and Mariel, Ian, and Julia Abbene. If my niece Shannon were old enough to read, I'm sure she would have made some valuable suggestions, too.

The following individuals shared expert advice related to pre-European human existence in Illinois and Chicago: William Iseminger (Cahokia Mounds State Historic Site), Linda Bechtle (Midwest Institute for Native American Studies), and Frances L. Hagemann. John Swenson reviewed and made helpful comments about the chapters on Chicago's early history, and Jerry Crimmins lent his expertise on Fort Dearborn.

Marc Lipkin at Alligator Records coordinated my interview with Koko Taylor. Thanks, Koko, for the great tips on the craft of writing a blues song.

Kenan Heise provided many of the wonderful photos that appear in this book.

The librarians, archivists, and photo reproduction staff at the Newberry Library, Chicago History Museum, and The Art Institute of Chicago were very cooperative and helpful.

Thanks also to Corina Carusi, John Powell, Heather Malec, Trina Higgins, Rob Medina, Erin Tikovitsch, Edward Maldonado, Steve Nash, and Jean Linsner.

Lisa Reardon was my capable and thorough project editor. Thanks finally to my editor, Cynthia Sherry, who responded so enthusiastically to the suggestion that we work together on this book and who patiently tolerated the anxieties of a first-time author.

Finally, and most importantly, thank you to my wife, Geralyn, whose love and support made this work possible.

INTRODUCTION

IMAGINE YOU COULD transport yourself back in time more than 300 years to the year 1673. Now pretend that you were standing at the center of what would eventually become modern-day Chicago. What would you see? Well, first of all, you'd probably be ankle-deep in water. Back then the future site of Chicago was mostly low-lying marshland that often flooded in the spring.

In summer you would see tall-grass prairies dotted with colorful wildflowers. You would see beavers, foxes, wolves, deer, rodents, and frogs. But you obviously wouldn't see the Sears Tower, the Lincoln Park Zoo, the Museum of Science and Industry, or Wrigley Field.

In fact, you probably wouldn't even see any other people. Even though about three million people live within Chicago's boundaries today, back then the mushy, swampy soil may have provided a suitable habitat for wildlife, but not for humans. Various tribes of Native Americans—Illinois, Miami, Potawatomi, Fox, and Kickapoo—settled in the outlying areas from time to time, farming the drier lands farther from the lake and surrounding marshes. In the autumn months they would most likely head west to hunt buffalo and deer.

The land you are imagining is about what Chicago would have looked like in 1673. That's when two Frenchmen became the first non–Native Americans to visit the future city. The visitors were a priest named Jacques Marquette and an explorer named Louis Jolliet. They were followed by fur trappers and traders who were the first ones

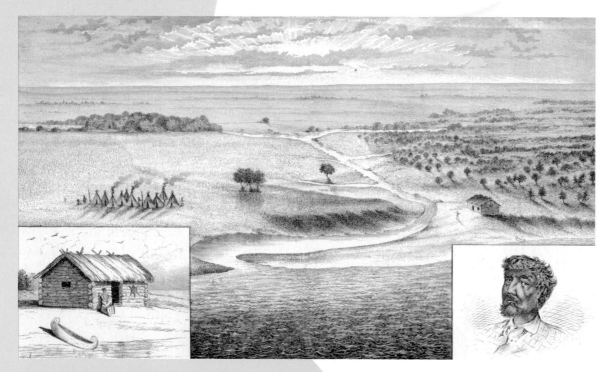

This drawing shows what Chicago may have looked like in the early 1780s.
HISTORY OF CHICAGO, A. T. ANDREAS COMPANY, 1884–86

to consider Chicago an ideal place to settle for good.

Ever since, Chicagoans have stopped at little to overcome nature's inconveniences. Unfortunately, progress has also had tragic consequences for the native peoples of this region, who lost their access to the land and with it their way of life. Modern life has also had damaging effects on the local wildlife and environment.

Still, Chicagoans are proud of the can-do attitude that helps them build some of the world's tallest skyscrapers, operate one of the world's busiest airports, and run the third-largest city in the United States. For better or worse, Chicago is always growing, changing, building, and inventing.

In the following pages, you can explore the city's streets and relive Chicago's most spectacular events. Imagine being the first explorer to set foot in Chicago. See what it was like to dodge the flames of the Great Chicago Fire. Take a ride on the world's first Ferris wheel. Along the way you can build a replica of Fort Dearborn, take walking tours of historic Chicago neighborhoods, and write a blues song.

A city of three million residents grew up around the once-deserted Chicago River.
PHOTO BY TERRY EVANS, *REVEALING CHICAGO*

1
Chicago Before Chicagoans

THE HISTORY OF CHICAGO goes back much further than the Chicago Fire, Chicago's World's Fairs, or the days of Al Capone. Many history books of Chicago start with the year 1673, when the first Europeans entered the area. This isn't one of those books. That's because the history of Chicago doesn't begin with the arrival of the European explorers and settlers. It didn't begin in 1492 either, when Christopher Columbus landed on the shores of the New World. By that time the American continents were already populated by millions of native peoples who had lived here for at least 9,000

An artist's conception of what the Chicago area might have looked like 16,000 years ago.
PAINTING BY ROBERT G. LARSON, COURTESY OF THE ILLINOIS STATE MUSEUM

Time Line

3 million years ago	Ice Age begins
100,000 years ago	Ice sheet covers Chicago
20,000 years ago	Chicago area glaciers begin to melt and recede; humans inhabit North America; Lake Chicago covers much of the future city
11,500 years ago	Clovis people hunt mastodons with spears
10,000 years ago	Mastodons and other North American megafauna die out
8,400 years ago	Archaic Indians construct dugout canoes
2,600 years ago	Native Americans make pottery
A.D. 400	Bow and arrow developed
A.D. 700	Large-scale farming begins
A.D. 1050–1200	Mississippian Indians reach their peak at Cahokia
A.D. 1400	End of significant Cahokian society

years—probably much longer. The earliest migrants may have even arrived as far back as 20,000 or even 30,000 years ago.

But the history of Chicago doesn't begin 30,000 years ago, either. To understand the city that we know today, you have to look back even further in time, more than one billion years, to explore the area's ecology, then progress to its human history, starting with the technological, social, and cultural riches of Native American societies.

A BRIEF HISTORY OF A LONG TIME

For anyone who wants to know about Chicago and how it came to be the great city it is today, it helps to know a few things about the environment of Chicago and its surrounding area. Why is Illinois so flat? What makes it such good farmland? What created those slopes and ridges in the Chicago area? Where did Lake Michigan come from?

Did you know that the land that is now Illinois—miles upon miles of flat corn and soybean fields—was once made up of violent, spewing volcanoes? That was 1.5 billion years ago, before the American continents had broken free from the Eurasian land mass and drifted to their current positions. Over the eons, North

Cooler by the Lake

CHICAGOANS KNOW firsthand how Lake Michigan affects the city's weather. A winter coat is just as often required to attend a Cubs or Sox game played in April as it is for a Bears game played in December. Lake Michigan is often to blame for the area's harsh weather. Because the lake is so deep and massive—and because water is more dense than air—it takes longer for the water temperature to catch up with the air temperature. In the spring it's often 10 to 15 degrees cooler on the shores of Lake Michigan than it is inland. In fall and early winter it's the other way around. And in winter when moist air warmed by the lake drifts over land it mixes with the cooler air to create "lake-effect snow."

America was periodically flooded by the oceans. Then sea levels would drop again, exposing the continent to air.

Now fast-forward a billion years. Believe it or not, the land that would eventually be Chicago—home of long, cold winters—was more like a tropical jungle 500 million years ago. The region's lush tropical plants would eventually die out and become covered with layers of soil and minerals. Over millions of years, this partially decayed material was compacted, and turned into coal.

About 200 million years ago, the continents began to break apart and drift away from each other. By about one million years ago the continents had reached the positions and shapes we recognize today, but the climate was still very different. This was

the period of the Great Ice Age. From then until about 20,000 years ago, much of the northern Midwestern region of North America was covered by ice, as a series of ice sheets descended from the north down through Canada and into the northern Midwest. Each one of these glaciers—some up to a mile high—leveled the earth's surface like an enormous steamroller, which is why much of Illinois is so flat.

As glaciers pressed southward, a ridge of dirt and other materials piled up in front of it, like a crest of dough created by a rolling pin. When the ice stopped growing and began melting, piles of debris left a physical record of where it stopped. Geologists call the piles of material left behind by retreating glaciers *moraines*.

A series of moraines in Chicago run parallel to the coast of Lake Michigan.

As the last ice sheet began to melt and recede, about 20,000 years ago, it left behind the rich minerals that make Illinois' farms so productive. (The farms surrounding Chicago would eventually play a major role in Chicago's economic growth.) The melting glaciers also created a much more swollen version of what is now Lake Michigan. Referred to as Lake Chicago, this body of water covered most of current-day Chicago with water. About 1,500 years ago Lake Michigan's shorelines ended up pretty close to where they are now.

Chicago Landscape

Elevation: 578.5 feet above sea level

Area: 228 square miles

Lake shoreline: 29 miles

River frontage: 100+ miles

Latitude: 41° 59° N

Longitude: 87° 54° W

CHICAGO DEPARTMENT OF PLANNING AND DEVELOPMENT, 2004

Miniature Glaciers

Make your own miniature glacier and see how moraines are formed. (Adapted from a lesson plan created by the Illinois State Museum and funded by the Illinois State Board of Education)

YOU'LL NEED

Dirt (a bucketful from your backyard, or potting soil)

Large rectangular watertight plastic tub (12 inches by 16 inches or larger)

Disposable plastic container (if round, 6–8 inches diameter; if square, 6–8 inches per side)

Gravel (a handful or so)

Water

Freezer

If you are getting dirt from your backyard, make sure that it doesn't contain too much clay, mulch, or debris. Arrange a layer of dirt about three inches deep in the large plastic tub. Pack it down lightly and level the surface.

GRAVEL →

← WATER LINE

In the smaller plastic container, add enough gravel so that it is about one-fourth full. Tilt the container and tap it a few times to make the contents pile up to one side. Gently add water to almost full. Freeze overnight into a solid block of ice.

Remove the miniature glacier from the container and place it on top of the dirt at one end of the plastic tub (the "north" end). Make sure that the side of the glacier with the majority of the gravel is pointed toward the "south" end of plastic tub. Press down firmly and slide the glacier toward the south end of the tub, stopping a few inches from the end. A significant amount of dirt from the tub should pile up in front of the advancing glacier.

Place the tub in a warm, dry area. As the ice melts, material from the miniature glacier should form a mound, much like a miniature moraine.

FROM FROZEN TUNDRA TO FIRE-PRONE PRAIRIE

When the glaciers came to Chicago, they wiped out a budding spruce forest. After the ice melted, the spruce trees made a partial comeback. Sparsely populated by trees and low-lying vegetation, the terrain looked much like tundra climates in northern Canada and Alaska today. As temperatures warmed, evergreens were replaced by *deciduous* trees. That's the name for trees—such as elm, oak, and maple—whose leaves change colors and fall off each autumn and return again each spring.

Deciduous trees need lots of water. So when the climate in Chicago became drier about 10,000 years ago, the first prairies sprang up in areas where these trees could no longer thrive. The warm, dry climate was perfect for numerous varieties of prairie grass. Late-summer prairie fires—ignited by lightning or, later, by Native American hunters and farmers—kept the forests from intruding on the prairies.

In addition to forests and prairies, Chicago's other main ecological characteristic is marshland. Much of the ground exposed when Lake Chicago shrunk to the Lake Michigan level was very low, and the soil had a spongy character to it. Frequent seasonal flooding, as the lake and river waters spilled over into the plain, created a habitat suited to cattails and other reed-like plants. Remnants of the marshlands can be seen in the Calumet River basin on the southern end of Lake Michigan.

THE FIRST AMERICANS

To understand who the first Chicagoans were, you need to look back in time and follow the progress and travels of the first American inhabitants.

It's not clear when or how, but the first humans may have arrived in North America as early as 20,000 years ago. They might have walked across the Bering land bridge that once provided an all-terrain crossing from Siberia to North America. It's also possible that they traveled by boat along the shorelines or after the crossing became submerged by rising sea levels. Others suggest that people arrived by boat from Europe.

These first pioneers to the Americas, called *Paleo-Indians*, encountered large prehistoric creatures, called *megafauna*: mastodons, woolly mammoths, musk ox, and other large land mammals that have since become extinct. Archaeologists have found evidence that Paleo-Indian hunters used spears equipped with razor-sharp stone points to hunt these large creatures. They heaved these spears using slings called *atlatls*. Stone points dating back nearly 14,000 years have been found at many sites in the Chicago area. Mastodon skeletons have been found in the Chicago area too, along with mammoth skeletons just over the border of Wisconsin.

The earliest inhabitants of North America were hunters and gatherers. They lived a nomadic lifestyle, which means that instead of settling in any one place, they moved frequently, often in time with the

Diagonal Streets

MOST OF CHICAGO'S streets conform to an orderly pattern of north–south and east–west streets. But a handful of diagonal streets seem to mess up the neatness of the street grid system. Two of these streets, Clark Street and the appropriately named Ridge Avenue, follow high-ground ridgelines. These were former shorelines from when Lake Michigan's water levels were much higher than they are today. For centuries Native Americans took advantage of the higher, drier trails, as did the wagons and cars that followed.

"More than six thousand years before Christ was born in Bethlehem, at least four thousand years before Stonehenge was constructed in southwestern England, and more than three thousand years before the great pyramids were erected to honor the Pharaohs in Egypt, people had settled in the great river valleys of the American Middle West."

—FROM *KOSTER: AMERICANS IN SEARCH OF THEIR PREHISTORIC PAST* (1979) BY STUART STRUEVER AND FELICIA ANTONELLI HOLTON

seasons, following game or in search of wild fruits, vegetables, and nuts.

It wasn't until thousands of years later when these early Native Americans learned how to farm their own land and grow crops for food that they could settle in one place year round. By about 9,000 years ago, in other parts of the world some humans lived in what could be considered cities, equipped with long-term housing structures, farm-land, social classes, and religious customs. It was also at around this time that Native Americans, who were living in small villages, first used a flint woodworking tool called an *adze* to make dugout canoes. This new technology helped Native Americans travel to and trade with distant tribes.

THE FIRST ILLINOISANS

One of the most amazing archaeological sites in Illinois is the Koster site. Located in downstate Illinois, near where the Mississippi and Illinois Rivers meet, this area has been called the "Nile of North America." This nickname reflects the area's plentiful natural resources as well as the rich cultural developments that they nourished.

What makes the Koster site special is that each layer excavated reveals another era of human development in Illinois prior to European contact. Archaeologists working there and at other sites in Illinois have found spear points and other tools (6000 B.C.), some of North America's earliest house structures (5000 B.C.), and artistic creations such as pipes and masks (A.D. 1000).

Excavations at Koster have proven that the first organized societies in North America occurred about 4,000 years earlier than previously thought. Artifacts and other evidence indicate the presence of smart hunter-gatherers who worked together and learned how to find food in the wilderness. Anthropologist Stuart Struever says that early Illinoisans could get food "with almost

Stone points like this would have been attached to a wooden shaft to make a spear used to hunt mastodons.
COURTESY OF THE ILLINOIS STATE MUSEUM

5

as much confidence as we drive to the supermarket for ours."

Archaeologists have pieced together what these people ate and how they prepared their meals. Their diets included plenty of protein, which they got from fish, deer, birds, and nuts. These early Illinoisans enjoyed such plentiful wild food supplies that for thousands of years they did not need to learn how to farm. Instead, they made steady improvements in their fishing and hunting techniques. They did begin farming around 5,000 years ago and expanded and improved those crops over the millennia. They were cultivating squash, gourds, sunflower, marshelder, erect knotweed, maygrass, little barley, and lamb's-quarter. The multitude of seeds they produced could be ground into flour or used in cooking. The bow and arrow was invented around A.D. 400, greatly improving hunting strategies. At about the same time, Native Americans were making advances in processing, preserving, and storing foods.

Large-scale farming of corn and squash began around A.D. 800–900. This new advance was probably a result of population growth. In turn, it probably led to even more increases in population as food surpluses could be provided and stored to feed larger, more permanent communities. This period also marks a major shift in the

How to Make a Dugout Canoe

DON'T TRY THIS ONE at home. Early Americans made canoes out of whole tree trunks. Because they didn't have saws or other machines, they had to find a different way to dig the wood out of the large, dense tree trunks. They used fire to burn a section of the log and then soaked it in water, making it softer. The next step was to dig out the burned section with an adze, which was similar to an axe made from a sharpened stone but attached at a right angle to a wooden handle.

relationship between Native Americans and the earth. Instead of just taking what nature offered, human beings were now changing nature to suit their needs.

THE FIRST "CAPITAL" OF ILLINOIS

Today, Springfield is the capital of Illinois, and Chicago is the state's largest city. But the first major political, economic, and cultural center in Illinois was located in Cahokia, Illinois, just northeast of present-day St. Louis. In A.D. 1050, Cahokia had a population of about 10,000–20,000, about the same as London at the time. Just like most big cities, Cahokia had big buildings, in this case built atop dirt mounds that could be seen from miles away.

The largest pyramid at Cahokia is called Monks Mound. It's the biggest dirt pyramid ever constructed in the Western Hemisphere. The only pre-European structures in the Americas that are larger are the stone pyramids of Mexico at Teotihuacán and Cholula.

In addition to the architectural and geometric knowledge needed to create this wondrous walled city, excavations of Cahokia show an advanced society complete with division of labor, political organization, religious customs, and business practices that would be familiar to modern people. These people traded raw materials and manufactured goods with faraway tribes. They produced art. They worshiped spirits and wondered about the possibility of an afterlife. They studied astronomy.

An artist's rendition of what Cahokia may have looked like at its peak.

Cahokia society also shared something in common with all sophisticated societies: social class divisions—the idea that different people play different roles depending on their skills and stature. Social divisions make monumental building projects possible, but they also create tension between the rulers and the ruled. As you study the history of Chicago, you'll see how these same tensions play out over and over throughout the years.

Scientists have estimated the amount of labor required to build the Cahokia Mounds, as well as the individual homes built upon and around them. It would have taken a crew of 3,000 at least two years to build Monks Mound alone. However, it was not built all at once, but in a series of stages over about 300 years. Most mounds that have been excavated exhibit several construction stages.

Artifacts found at the Cahokia site give us a pretty good idea of how the people of that time lived. Spear points, arrowheads, knives, scrapers, and fishhooks indicate hunting and fishing. Hoes made from shells

All Work and No Play

NATIVE AMERICAN populations who lived at the Cahokia Mounds played a sport called chunkey. Two competitors standing side by side would each throw a spear at a stone disk rolled away from them. The spear landing closest to where the disk stopped was the winner. Another early game has been referred to as corn darts. Similar to modern-day lawn darts, the projectiles were made by fixing a stone point to the narrow end of a corn cob and feathers to the opposite end. These darts were then tossed at a target ring made of corn husks tied together.

attached to the ends of sticks were used for small digging jobs. Bigger jobs, like tilling farmland or building mounds, were done with large flint hoes tied onto sturdy wood handles with rawhide. Bone needles were used for sewing clothes and other materials.

Nobody knows why, but the civilization at Cahokia Mounds died out around A.D. 1400. The cause may have been a war with other tribes, disease, failing corn crops, depletion of resources, or other environmental factors. Maybe the inhabitants divided into smaller groups and settled elsewhere, establishing new villages or going to those

where they had relatives. Whatever the reason, Cahokia Mounds was the last major pre-European urban settlement in Illinois.

The Native Americans who inhabited the areas surrounding the future site of Chicago, in Illinois, Wisconsin, Indiana, and Michigan, did not create long-term settlements like Cahokia. Instead they lived in societies that some have called semisedentary. *Sedentary* means staying still or in one place. Various groups of Native Americans set up temporary camps or villages in the Chicago area, but also traveled to other areas throughout the year to hunt and trade.

Bean Bag Chunkey

Substitute bean bags for spears and you too can play this ancient game, probably one of the first sports played in the Midwest region of North America.

YOU'LL NEED

2 players

1 judge

1 hockey puck

2 bean bags (preferably different colors in order to tell players apart)

Tape measure

This game should be played in an open space, like a gymnasium or park.

Three people line up facing the same direction. The person in the middle (the judge) rolls the hockey puck on its edge in the direction that all three players are facing. On a count of three, the two other players simultaneously throw their bean bags toward the spot that they think the hockey puck will stop. The player whose bean bag is closest to the hockey puck's resting point wins.

As you practice you will get better at judging how far the puck will go and how far to throw the bean bag. If you're playing on a slick surface, like a gymnasium floor, it might help to throw the bean bag higher in the air, to reduce the distance it slides once it hits the floor.

This statue, made about 700 years ago, shows a man preparing to roll a chunkey stone.

PHOTO BY JOHN BIGELOW TAYLOR, *HERO, HAWK AND OPEN HAND*, COURTESY OF ST. LOUIS SCIENCE CENTER

2

The First Chicagoans

SURPRISINGLY, WE ACTUALLY know less today about the more recent populations of Native Americans than we do about the people who lived here much longer ago. Partly, that's because of the different lifestyles they led. Long-term settlements, like the ones found at Koster and Cahokia, produced more artifacts to study. Houses, fire pits, cemeteries, and even garbage heaps provide clues to how the earlier Native Americans lived.

It seems as if Illinois's Native American populations from the 1400s to the 1670s adopted a more mobile lifestyle. They were

Time Line	
900–1600	Bowmanville Native American village active
1300–1600	Blue Island culture inhabits southwest Cook County
1600	Miami Indians occupy most of future site of Chicago; Potawatomi Indians live in western Michigan
1673	First European explorers arrive in Chicago
1700	Potawatomi move south from Wisconsin, settle in Chicago area

This detail of the Blue Island community is from a map of Indian villages and trails made by Albert Scharf. Some have questioned the way Scharf did his research, but the map still provides a good idea of how and where the Native Americans lived in Chicago before Europeans.

AUTHOR'S COLLECTION

What's in a Name?

THE CITY AND DOWNTOWN river most likely got their name from the word *Checagou*, which was an Algonquin word meaning "striped skunk." The name was later applied to the river because of the skunky odor produced by the wild garlic plants growing on the banks of the Chicago River. Over the years Chicagoans have tried to come up with a more respectable story about the origin of the city's name. Some have claimed Chicago was named after a Native American chief of the same name, but that's not likely. There's no evidence linking Checagou the chief, who lived in present-day Missouri, with the name used for the Chicago River or Chicago the city.

frequently on the move, and so they left a more scattered record of their existence. Also, their culture produced no written records. For thousands of years Native Americans maintained an oral tradition. Instead of writing down their history and beliefs, they passed them along from generation to generation through stories told to each other.

But it seems there were a few substantial pre-European settlements in the Chicago region. A site northwest of today's Loop, called the Bowmanville site, was active from 900 to 1600. The Blue Island culture, to the southwest of modern-day downtown Chicago, was active from 1300 to 1600.

Archaeologists have unearthed evidence of sturdy houses and artistic relics such as pipes and masks, as well as pottery reinforced with crushed mussel shells.

With so little archaeological evidence to study, the only other information available about the Native Americans comes from oral history, the stories they told for centuries. Native Americans continue to pass along their stories today. Some of them have recently been written down.

There were about six different Native American tribes that resided in the area surrounding what would eventually become Chicago. The Illinois, Miami, Potawatomi, Kickapoo, Fox, and Mascouten were all part of the larger Algonquin language family of Native Americans, sharing similar languages and customs.

The big question is, how many Native Americans lived in this area? It's impossible to know for sure, because estimates made by the first Europeans differ significantly. Some have estimated that there were as many as 100,000 Native Americans living in the entire Great Lakes region. In 1600 about 20,000 Native Americans were said to be living on the land surrounding the bottom half of Lake Michigan. Many of them were Illinois Indians, who had ranged north from central Illinois. The Illinois suffered huge losses in wars with the Iroquois. The next tribe to settle in the area was the Miami, followed by the Kickapoos, and finally the Potawatomi.

The earlier Native Americans who lived in this region split their time between Chicago, where they grew corn and then stored it in underground cellars, and the Western Plains where they moved to hunt buffalo in the autumn months. When they were in the Chicago area, they hunted deer, bears, turkeys, geese, ducks, and swans. They also fished the local rivers and lakes and supplemented their diets with wild vegetables, roots, berries, and nuts.

INDIAN TRAILS
AND
VILLAGES OF CHICAGO
AND OF
COOK, DUPAGE AND
WILL COUNTIES, ILLS.
(1804)
AS SHOWN BY
WEAPONS AND IMPLEMENTS
OF THE STONE-AGE.
COPYRIGHTED
1900 & 1901
ALBERT F. SCHARF.

— INDEX —
INDIAN VILLAGES, (NUMBERED.)
MINOR INDIAN VILLAGES
INDIAN CAMPS
CHIPPING STATIONS
PRINCIPAL INDIAN TRAILS
LETTERED AND NUMBERED
PORTAGE
SPRINGS
HEIGHTS AND
SIGNAL STATIONS
INDIAN MOUNDS

MOUND BUILDERS
TRAIL

SCALE OF MAP
5/16 IN. TO MILE.

The Bowmanville community as depicted on the Scharf map.

AUTHOR'S COLLECTION

In the late winter or early spring, the Native Americans would return to their Chicago-area homes and live off the fruits of their hunting and farming activities while planning for the next planting season.

TEPEES, WIGWAMS, AND LONGHOUSES

Many people might think that the Native Americans who lived in this area lived in tepees. But most of the people living in Northern Illinois constructed more durable homes to withstand the harsh Midwestern weather that today's Chicagoans still complain about. According to a priest who visited the Illinois Indians, "the cabins of the more northerly Illinois were made like long arbors covered with double mats of reeds, so well sowed that neither wind nor rain nor snow could penetrate." Vents were built into the roof to release the smoke from fires.

The Potawatomi tribe of Native Americans is the one most closely associated with Chicago because they were the most recent American Indian occupants of the area. Sometime in the early 1600s the Potawatomi moved from Michigan to Wisconsin. By 1700 they had moved south to the Chicago area, where they lived for the next 130 years. The Potawatomi's experiences with the white European settlers started out fairly well, as they traded and lived side-by-side with the French trappers and traders, called *voyageurs*. Later, though, their relations with the British and Americans became more complicated and less friendly.

But it almost didn't matter which Europeans the Great Lakes Indians befriended and which ones they went to war with. It was the European way of life that forever altered the Native American way of life in this area. Once Native Americans engaged in trade with the Europeans, they headed down a new path. Many Great

After the Hunt

IN A SUCCESSFUL HUNT, Native Americans may have killed up to 200 buffalo. But how did they transport their kills back to their villages? And how did they keep the meat from spoiling? Because a full-grown buffalo can weigh up to 2,000 pounds, there was no way to transport it back to the village in one piece. Instead, the animals were butchered on the spot, dried, and smoked, like beef jerky. The lighter loads were easier to transport and they didn't spoil as quickly.

Chicago's First Sport

BEFORE THE CUBS, White Sox, Bears, Bulls, and Blackhawks ever played a game in the city, the first sport played in the Chicago area was lacrosse, a game that is now played as a high school and collegiate sport. In his study of Native Americans living in the Chicago area, William Strong said that lacrosse "was a brutal sport, and many people were seriously crippled by being hit over the legs with the heavy rackets or by the solid wood ball." Lacrosse may have been a way for rival Native American communities to settle disputes without resorting to full-scale warfare.

This is an example of the kind of pottery that was made by Chicago-area Native Americans before they started trading with the Europeans.
COURTESY OF THE ILLINOIS STATE MUSEUM

Lakes Indians became dependent on the Europeans for clothing, blankets, cookware, knives, guns, tobacco, and liquor. It was easier for them to trade otter and beaver skins for these items than it was to continue with their old ways of doing things. Some of the groups who no longer practiced their traditions eventually forgot them. For example, it was at about this time that the art of pottery making was lost to the people of the Great Lakes.

The first Europeans arrived in Chicago in 1673. Just 160 years later, the Native Americans would be evicted from the land they had farmed and hunted for thousands of years.

Construct a Model Longhouse

Using materials found at a craft store, you can construct a small-scale version of a Native American longhouse.

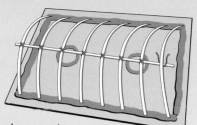

YOU'LL NEED

Ruler

Scissors

10 strips of ¼ x 36-inch balsa wood

Poster board (20 x 30 inches, preferably white)

Modeling clay (one package, preferably brown)

8 garbage bag twist ties

Brown felt (enough to make one 18 x 12-inch rectangle)

1. Using your ruler and scissors, measure and cut one 19-inch length of balsa wood. This piece will form the top (or apex) of the longhouse.

2. Cut 16 different 15-inch pieces of balsa wood. You'll need eight pieces to form the arches of the longhouse. Keep the extras to replace arches that might accidentally snap during construction.

3. Cut the poster board in half on the long side to make two pieces of 15 inches by 20 inches. Set one half aside.

4. Form the modeling clay into four "snakes"— two of them 12 inches long and two that are 18 inches long.

5. Place the clay snakes onto the illustration board so as to form a rectangle that's 12 inches by 18 inches. Press the snakes flat on the illustration board.

6. Roll out two more thinner snakes about 5 inches long each. Join the two ends to form a circle. Place these on the poster board, 4½ inches from the 12-inch clay sides.

7. At 3-inch intervals, insert one end of each arch into the clay along one of the 18-inch clay sides. One by one, gently bend each of the arches enough to insert the other end into the clay at the opposite 18-inch clay side. (Note: Balsa wood is very brittle. Expect some pieces to snap during construction, no matter how careful you are. Just select another piece and try again. If you find this too frustrating, consider substituting with another material, maybe plastic strips.)

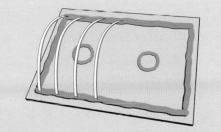

8. Lay the 19-inch apex piece across the top of the arches. Using the garbage bag twist ties, attach the apex to each of the arches.

9. Cut the felt into a rectangle with dimensions of 19 inches by 15 inches. Fold the felt in half the long way to make a 19 x 7½-inch rectangle. Cut two semicircles at the fold line (make sure the center point of the resulting circle is about 5 inches from the edge, so that these smoke vents will line up with the firepits).

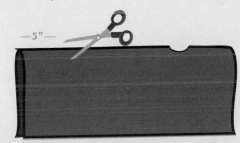
—5"—

10. Unfold the felt and drape it over the balsa frame.

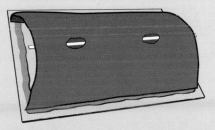

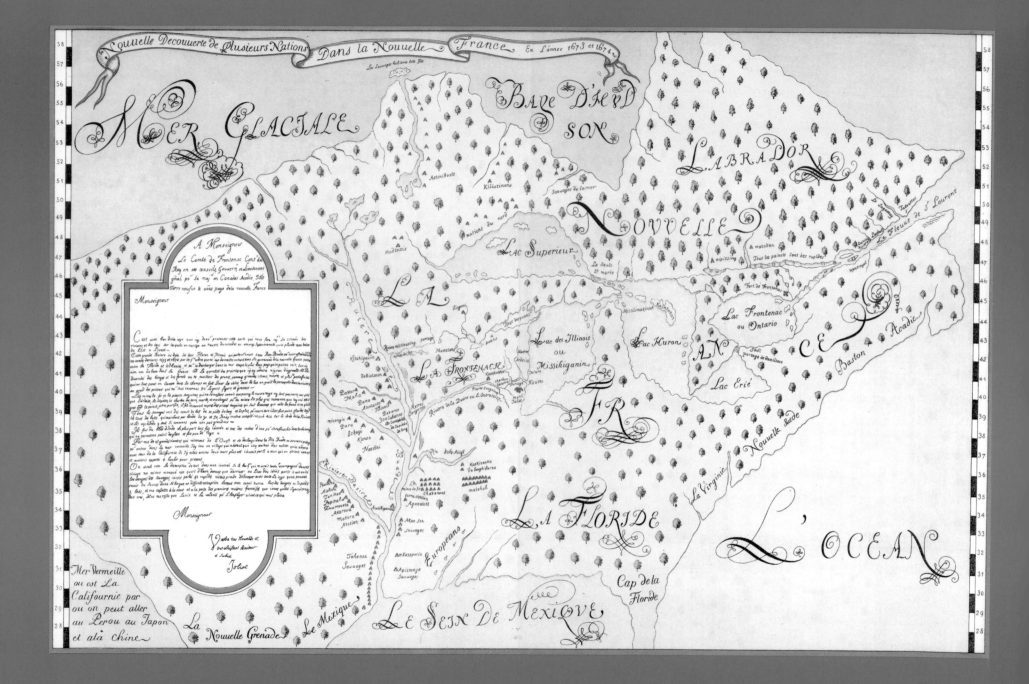

3
Explorers, Missionaries, Trappers, and Soldiers

NATIVE AMERICANS NEVER REALLY considered the swampy, marshy land near where the Chicago River met Lake Michigan a good place to live. They preferred the higher, drier ground to the northwest and southwest. But from the first time they laid eyes on it, Europeans thought the area had great potential. To some extent, this was due to a difference in economic systems. Native Americans lived

This map of North America was drawn by French explorer Louis Jolliet after he and fellow Frenchman Jacques Marquette became the first Europeans to explore the region that would eventually come to be called Chicago.

HISTORY OF CHICAGO, A. I. ANDREAS COMPANY, 1884–86

Time Line

1673	Louis Jolliet and Jacques Marquette "discover" Chicago
1754–63	French and Indian War
1776	Declaration of Independence published
1782	Jean Baptiste Point Du Sable moves to Chicago
1783	Treaty of Paris: British surrender territory including future site of Chicago
1795	Treaty of Greenville: Indians grant future site of Chicago to the United States
1800	Jean Baptiste Point Du Sable sells his property, moves south
1803	Fort Dearborn erected
1804	John Kinzie and family move into Point Du Sable's house
1812	Fifteen permanent residences in Chicago; War of 1812; Fort Dearborn Massacre
1813	Tecumseh killed by U.S. forces
1816	Native Americans cede claims to land southwest of Chicago
1818	Illinois becomes a state
1825	Erie Canal opens
1832	Black Hawk War

in small, tight-knit communities that lived off the land. They hunted for, grew, and gathered the items needed to feed, clothe, and shelter themselves. Although they engaged in trade with tribes from all over North America, Native Americans did not use money. As a result, Native Americans rarely needed to produce more than they themselves needed.

European society, on the other hand, had developed a mercantile society. Different people specialized in different professions. Some were farmers, some were skilled crafts-people who, for example, made furniture or hats made from animal fur. Instead of the barter system in which people traded one type of good or service for another, the European economy was based on currency, or money.

Currency-based economies created new economic classes, such as merchants, who bought and sold goods, and capitalists, who financed the large-scale manufacture of goods. At the bottom of the economic ladder was unskilled labor, the workers who were at the mercy of market forces and the whims of their employers.

THE EUROPEANS ARE COMING

By the 1670s Europe's economy was rather sophisticated. Goods were being traded all

Jacques Marquette (1637–1675).
COURTESY OF KENAN HEISE

Louis Jolliet (1645–1700).
COURTESY OF KENAN HEISE

over the known world. The French were the first to expand trade west toward central Canada and the Great Lakes region. Raw materials—especially beaver pelts—collected in the Great Lakes region were being shipped east and sometimes all the way back to Europe. Manufactured goods were being shipped in the opposite direction to markets being developed in the New World.

One of the keys to a far-flung, currency-based economy is transportation—the ability to ship materials and goods afford-ably from one location to another. Plentiful

raw materials and transportation are what made Chicago's location attractive to Europeans.

The first two Europeans to discover Chicago in 1673 were French—a Catholic missionary priest named Father Jacques Marquette and an explorer named Louis Jolliet. But why were they venturing into these unknown lands? What were they looking for? And how did their arrival mark the beginning of the end of a way of life that had existed on this continent for approximately 10,000 years?

HIDES AND SOULS

Two driving forces motivated the French to explore the region: money and religion. Jolliet was sent into the wilderness to see if the area had plentiful raw materials (like beaver pelts and bison hides), to map out travel and trade routes, and to forge trade relationships with the native people. Father Marquette's mission was to convert the "savages" into Christians. Both were successful to a degree. But success for the Europeans would eventually spell disaster for the Native Americans.

About 130 years before the more famous duo of Meriweather Lewis and William Clark began their journey of exploration, Marquette and Jolliet pushed their canoes off the shores of St. Ignace, Michigan. Accompanied by five explorers, they traveled down the west coast of Lake Michigan to Green Bay, where they paddled down rivers flowing into the Mississippi. Reaching the future site of modern-day Peoria, they encountered a Native American village of Miami Indians.

After establishing a mission, Marquette and Jolliet continued south, eventually getting as far as Arkansas, where they were befriended by a tribe of Kaskaskia Indians. But Marquette fell ill, and the French explorers decided to return north to the St. Ignace mission. A group of Kaskaskia

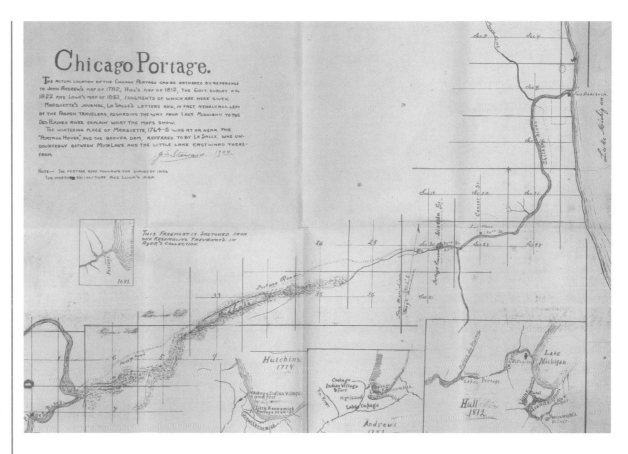

This map shows the distance that Marquette and Jolliet would have had to carry their canoes—about six miles.

THE NEWBERRY LIBRARY

escorted the European explorers for a portion of their return journey. They also suggested a shortcut: to take the Illinois River northeast toward Lake Michigan. This route was more direct, but it also forced the explorers to make a short portage—to carry their canoes and supplies over land.

In his journal Jolliet was the first to note that digging a canal there would complete the

Part Lake, Part River, Part Time

AT CERTAIN TIMES of the year, the ground between the Des Plaines and Chicago Rivers would be flooded, making it unnecessary to portage. During spring a shallow and sluggish body of water called Mud Lake could accommodate small crafts. A reliable all-water passage from Chicago to the Gulf of Mexico would come 175 years later, when the Illinois & Michigan Canal connected the Des Plaines and Illinois Rivers in 1848.

all-water passage from Canada to the Gulf of Mexico. "It would only be necessary," Jolliet mused, "to cut a canal by cutting through but half a league of prairie from the foot of the Lake of Illinois [Lake Michigan] to the river Saint Louis [Illinois River]."

Once back at the St. Ignace mission, Marquette was nursed back to health. The following year he kept his promise and returned to preach to his new flock of Native American followers. Unfortunately, he again became seriously ill and decided to return north after only a short stay at the Kaskaskia village. While making his return trip to the mission at St. Ignace, Michigan, Marquette died on the eastern shores of Lake Michigan, near present-day Ludington, Michigan.

Jolliet never returned to Chicago, but that didn't stop future Europeans from coming or the fur trade from changing life on the prairies.

THE FUR TRADE

European fur trappers and traders quickly followed Marquette and Jolliet's travels south. The region was full of fur-bearing animals, which were trapped, skinned, and transported east by boat. For the most part, these voyageurs got along well with the Native Americans and paid them for the beaver pelts they trapped. Native Americans didn't know it at the time, but by participating in the fur trade, they willingly cooperated in undoing their old way of life.

Native Americans harvested the raw materials (pelts) and traded them to the white settlers for products manufactured in Europe and on the East Coast of America: clothing, food, whiskey, and guns. They eventually began using European money. In doing so, they joined the European

mercantile society. They became dependent on others to provide not only the luxuries they came to desire but also everyday necessities, such as pots and pans, knives, saws, and axes. Native Americans steadily abandoned their old ways of life.

The Potawatomi tribe of Native Americans had mostly lived peacefully alongside the first French settlers. Partly this was because only small numbers of French ever migrated to the area. But in

Voyageurs like the one in this drawing by Frederic Remington lived in the Great Lakes regions of North America.
COURTESY OF KENAN HEISE

the mid-1700s the British were beginning to move into the region in larger numbers. The British were interested in taking trade and territory away from the French.

The French and Indian War of 1754–63 pitted the British against both the French and their Native American allies, including some groups of the Potawatomi. The British successfully ousted the French from the area, but that didn't mean that the war was over as far as the pro-French Potawatomi were concerned. They continued to sack British forts in the area, until a truce was reached in 1765. The Chicago region was now officially under British rule, but not for long.

During the American Revolution, most groups of Potawatomi took sides with the British against the American colonists. In the years following the war, many Potawatomi continued to resist American infiltration of the land. Some Chicago-area Potawatomi, on the other hand, sided with the Americans or stayed out of the conflicts altogether.

Warfare between the Native Americans and the Americans stopped for awhile in 1795, with the Treaty of Greenville. This treaty was an important turning point in the history of Chicago, because it was the first time some of the Great Lakes tribes formally signed away their rights to any property in the area. Specifically, they granted the United States "one piece of land, six miles square at or near the mouth of the Chicago River, emptying into the southwest end of Lake Michigan."

THE FOUNDER OF MODERN CHICAGO

Native Americans had, of course, lived in and around the present-day Chicago area off and on for thousands of years—as had a number of missionaries and voyageurs in the years after the first European explorations of the area. But the first known, long-term, non–American Indian resident of Chicago was Jean Baptiste Point Du Sable. No one knows for sure when or where Point Du Sable was born. Some say he was born in Haiti in 1745, of a French father and an African slave mother. Other evidence suggests he was born in Cahokia, Illinois, in 1740.

Before moving to Chicago, Point Du Sable had worked for various fur-trading interests in the Great Lakes regions. He spoke French, maybe a little English, and bits and pieces of several Indian languages. For years he traded furs among the Great Lakes Indians in present-day Indiana and Michigan. Then, sometime around 1782, Point Du Sable established a farm and

The French and Indian War

BEFORE THE REVOLUTIONARY WAR, future Americans like George Washington and Benjamin Franklin were still British subjects. As the population in the colonies increased, more and more British subjects moved west, seeking farmland and trade opportunities. But when they did, the colonists came into conflict with the Native Americans and the French. The French and Indian War broke out in 1754, after the 22-year-old Colonel George Washington lost Fort Necessity in what is now Pennsylvania to a combined force of French and Native American allies.

The British eventually won the war and by 1763 claimed all territory in the Great Lakes region east of the Mississippi River. But the colonists felt like they did most of the fighting, while the British made most of the decisions. These conflicts were the first signs that the colonists would not live quietly under British rule.

trading post on the north bank of the Chicago River, not far from where the Michigan Avenue bridge now spans the river. He seems to have made a prosperous living, mostly by farming, but also by trading between the Native Americans and the French voyageurs. His marriage to a Potawatomi woman no doubt assisted in his trade with the Native Americans.

By the time Point Du Sable sold his farm and equipment in 1800 and eventually moved to Missouri, he was a relatively wealthy man. The bill of sale shows that he

This is an artist's rendition of what Chicago may have looked like at about the time when Jean Baptiste Point Du Sable lived just north of the river. Notice the animal pelt pinned to his house, a sign to nearby Indians that they could trade their animal pelts here.

HISTORY OF CHICAGO, A. T. ANDREAS COMPANY, 1884–86

Street Cred

THE KINZIE FAMILY may hold the record for most Chicago streets named in their honor. Ellen Street and Marion Court are both named for Ellen Marion Kinzie, who was the first European child born in Chicago, in 1804. Eleanor Street was named for her mother; and Kinzie Street was named after her father, John Kinzie, who moved into the house built by Jean Baptiste Point Du Sable in 1804. Another early Chicagoan, Ellen's first husband, Dr. Alexander Wolcott, is the namesake for Wolcott Avenue.

had amassed an impressive collection of property, which he sold for what was then a large sum of money.

The next famous resident of that property was John Kinzie, who bought the property in 1804. At various times of his life, Kinzie was a silversmith, fur trader, farmer, and merchant. Most of his customers were soldiers and officers who moved into the area when Fort Dearborn was built.

FORT DEARBORN

At this time, the future site of Chicago wasn't much more than a one-horse town. There were only four permanent residences.

A painting of the construction of the original Fort Dearborn, built in 1803.

COURTESY OF KENAN HEISE

The largest and most significant structures in the town were in Fort Dearborn. Built in 1803 to protect Americans living and trading in the area, it became the westernmost military outpost of the United States.

In April 1803 Captain John Whistler arrived in Chicago with six men to survey the land and plan the building of Fort Dearborn. Four months later, Whistler returned to Chicago with 68 soldiers, as well as his wife and three children. By winter, construction of the barracks and two blockhouses was finished. For the next eight years Fort Dearborn and its occupants lived in relative peace with the Potawatomi and other native people of the area.

Fort Dearborn also sent a message to the British, who were still clinging to the

Revising History

SOME EARLY HISTORIANS didn't like the idea that Chicago's "founding father" was a black man. The author of the following excerpt from *Chicago and Its Distinguished Citizens*, published in 1881, preferred to think of Marquette as the first white settler—even though the priest only passed through the area.

> All that Jean Baptiste Point Du Sable did for Chicago, was to build a hut and then desert it. He was the type of modern tramphood—aimless, shiftless, useless. Marquette came for a purpose, braved danger to accomplish it, and left only when duty called him to another field.

But attitudes change. By 1933 organizers of the Century of Progress Chicago World's Fair were touting Point Du Sable as "Chicago's First Citizen." In 1963 Mayor Richard J. Daley and the Chicago City Council officially recognized Point Du Sable as "the first Chicago resident of record" and declared August 18–24 "Du Sable Week in Chicago." And in 1987, a United States Post Office stamp was issued in Point Du Sable's honor.

Build a Replica of Fort Dearborn

Named after President Abraham Lincoln, Lincoln Logs were invented in 1916 by then 25-year-old John Lloyd Wright (second son of the world-famous architect Frank Lloyd Wright). You can use Lincoln Logs to make your own version of Fort Dearborn.

YOU'LL NEED

1 set of Lincoln Logs

Popsicle sticks (100 or so)

Washable wood glue

Rubber bands or garbage bag twist ties

Assorted plastic toy soldiers and horses

Study the illustration below and create your own version of Fort Dearborn using the Lincoln Logs.

To build the fence surrounding the log buildings, lay six Popsicle sticks vertically on a flat surface. Then overlay two Popsicle sticks horizontally. Adjust the number of vertical Popsicle sticks so that the horizontal Popsicle sticks extend beyond the vertical ones slightly. Glue the horizontal sticks across the vertical ones. Repeat this process, making as many wall panels as you think you might need.

To connect panels, glue the top and bottom horizontal sticks of one panel to another. At corners you can attach the horizontal flaps with rubber bands or garbage bag twist ties. Make a perimeter around the buildings in the fort.

Man your fort with toy soldiers and horses.

This cartoon shows a British soldier paying a Native American for the scalp of an American citizen.
LIBRARY OF CONGRESS, LC-USZ62-5800

regions west of official U.S. territory. When Ohio became the 17th state in 1803, the western U.S. border ran along the Ohio River. Illinois—which was at the time referred to as the Northwest Territory—would not become a state for another 15 years, and the British stood to lose much by clearing out.

By providing some Native Americans groups with favors, goods, and promises to help them retain or regain their lands, the British encouraged native hostility toward the Americans, who were now the biggest threat to their existence. The tension resulted in several skirmishes, the biggest one being the 1811 Battle of Tippecanoe in which U.S. forces under William Henry

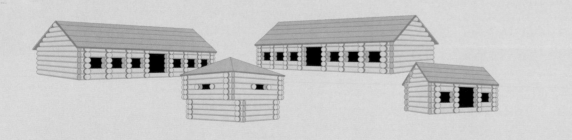

Harrison beat back a Shawnee attack, sacking and burning much of the Indians' nearby village.

By the time the War of 1812 broke out between the British and the United States, with some Native Americans taking the British side, it was no longer safe at Fort Dearborn. On August 9 General William Hull sent orders to Fort Dearborn commandant Captain Nathan Heald to abandon Fort Dearborn and retreat to Fort Wayne. Unfortunately, things didn't go as planned.

FORT DEARBORN MASSACRE

Before the U.S. forces left Fort Dearborn, they were visited by a band of Potawatomi who offered to escort the soldiers and their families to safety. Captain Heald didn't trust the Potawatomi, but he also didn't want them

This map shows the location of Fort Dearborn and a few nearby residences (lower right), as well as the location of the Fort Dearborn Massacre (lower left).

Tecumseh Takes a Stand

THE SHAWNEE WARRIOR Tecumseh rightly saw the construction of Fort Dearborn as a sign of the white man's aggressive intentions. He spoke eloquently in recruiting other tribes to join his Western Confederacy, an armed resistance to white settlement:

Before me stand the rightful owners of *kwaw-notchi-we au-kee* [this beautiful land]. The Great Spirit in His wisdom gave it to you and your children to defend, and placed you here. But, *ä-te-wä!* [alas!] the incoming race, like a huge serpent, is coiling closer and closer about you. And not content with hemming you in on every side, they have built at *She-gog-ong* [Chicago], in the very centre of our country, a military fort, garrisoned with soldiers, ready and equipped for battle. As sure as *waw-kwen-og* [the heavens] are above you they are determined to destroy you and your children and occupy this goodly land themselves.

—quoted by Potawatomi Chief Simon Pokagon, in *Harper's New Monthly Magazine*, March 1899

Just Lucky?

WHY DID THE POTAWATOMI spare the life of John Kinzie and his family? As the son of British subjects, John Kinzie took sides with the British at first, but he also earned his living by doing business with the Americans living at Fort Dearborn. From 1807 to 1809, and again in 1812, Kinzie had an exclusive contract to supply the Fort Dearborn soldiers with goods. Some have suggested that Kinzie was a double-agent, playing the British, Americans, and Potawatomi against each other. Earlier in 1812 Kinzie killed Jean Lalime, an Indian interpreter working for the U.S. government. Some think Kinzie's dispute with Lalime was due to a long-standing personal or business quarrel. Others said that Lalime may have been planning to expose Kinzie's anti–U.S. activities to the officers at Fort Dearborn. Shortly before Fort Dearborn was attacked in 1812, Kinzie attended a British-sponsored meeting of Native Americans, so he may have known about the attack ahead of time and made a deal with the Potawatomi.

This imaginative painting of the Fort Dearborn Massacre reflects the American settlers' version of the event.
COURTESY OF KENAN HEISE

to know that. So he accepted their offer and promised to let the Potawatomi have the ammunition, rifles, and supplies left behind by the departing Americans. Instead, Captain Heald ordered his men to dump the fort's weapons and whiskey into the Chicago River.

On the morning of August 15, 1812, the entire group of Americans—66 to 68 U.S. soldiers and militia, nine women, and 18 children—left Fort Dearborn and headed south along the Lake Michigan shore. They were accompanied by a small force of Miami Indians along with Captain William Wells, who had rushed to Chicago from Fort Wayne, Indiana, to oversee the safety of his niece Rebekah Heald (wife of Captain

Captain William Wells

CAPTAIN WILLIAM WELLS, uncle of Rebekah Heald, led an adventurous life. Kidnapped by Miami Indians at a young age, he grew up as the adopted son of Miami chief Little Turtle. Eventually he returned to live among white Americans, even facing off against Native Americans in warfare. During the Fort Dearborn Massacre, Wells fought bravely, but he did not survive the attack. Because of his reputation as a courageous warrior, Wells' heart was cut out of his body by the Potawatomi.

Heald). Following a lakefront trail, the Americans were ambushed two miles south of the fort by a force of about 500 Potawatomi hidden behind the Lake Michigan sand dunes. Angered by Heald's double-cross, and fighting for the preservation of their land and culture, the Potawatomi fought fiercely and mercilessly. By the time the fighting was over, more than 60 Americans were dead, including two women and 12 children. Survivors included Captain Heald, his wife Rebekah, and the Kinzie family, who had enjoyed a long and mostly positive relationship with the Potawatomi.

As horrifying as this military defeat was, in the long run the Fort Dearborn Massacre did little to stem the tide of U.S. occupation of the Midwest. Tecumseh was killed in the following year by U.S. forces led by General William Henry Harrison. When Britain lost the War of 1812 to the United States, the Native Americans lost an important and powerful ally in their battle with the United States. Four years later in 1816, the U.S. military rebuilt Fort Dearborn, returning stability to the region, as far as the white settlers were concerned.

WHEN THE CITY WAS STILL COUNTRY

In the 1820s and 1830s life in Chicago was more like living on a farm than in a city—no surprise, considering that there were only a handful of residents. A government mission sent to survey the area brought a young man named Henry Schoolcraft to Chicago in August 1820. In addition to making a sketch of the settlement, Schoolcraft studied the farming potential of the outlying areas. "As a farming country," Schoolcraft suggested, "it presents the greatest facilities for raising stock and grains. . . . The climate has a delightful serenity, and it must, as soon as the Indian title is extinguished, become one of the most attractive fields for the emigrant."

Schoolcraft also noticed what Jolliet had 150 years earlier, that Chicago could serve as "a depot for the commerce between the northern and southern sections of the Union, and a great thoroughfare for strangers, merchants, and travelers." But that would have to wait for the completion of canals that would make it easier to transport goods throughout the Midwest. The Erie Canal connected New York to Lake Erie in 1825, and the Illinois & Michigan Canal fulfilled Jolliet's vision in 1848. These two developments would eventually bring farmers, real estate developers, factories, and all the money needed to build up the city.

But that was more than a decade away. Back in 1820 Chicagoans were still too occupied with the realities and hardships of day-to-day life to imagine Chicago's future importance to the young country. After passing through the area at about this time, a messenger and trader named John H. Fonda was less impressed than Schoolcraft. "It never occurred to me that

Walking/Bus Tour: Chicago's Oldest Landmarks

Did you know that you can visit the original location of Chicago's Fort Dearborn? Stand where Jean Baptiste Point Du Sable lived? Tour a Chicago home that was built in 1836?

Start at the corner of Wacker Drive and Wabash Avenue. This plaza is called Heald Square (1), after Nathan Heald, the commander at Fort Dearborn in 1812. Walk northeast on Wacker toward Lake Michigan. Stop just before you reach Michigan Avenue. You are now standing where Fort Dearborn (2) once stood. Find one of the bronze markers embedded in the sidewalk, and follow the outline of the fort. Be careful crossing streets.

Next go to the Michigan Avenue Bridge (3) spanning the Chicago River. Notice the historical scenes sculptured into the bridge's four limestone pylons. (Seven more panels depicting early Chicago history can be found on the fifth floor façade at 333 N. Michigan Avenue.) Then cross the bridge and look back south. Imagine you are Jean Baptise Point Du Sable, gazing over the empty prairies, before any of these buildings were constructed.

In front of the Wrigley Building (4), catch a CTA #3 bus southbound to 18th Avenue (about 15 minutes). From there, walk one block east and take a right on Indiana Avenue. Half a block south on the east side of the street you'll find the Clarke House (5) at 1827 S. Indiana. Call ahead for a tour schedule (312-326-1480). From the Clarke House, walk back north to 18th Avenue and take a right.

One block east you'll find the Glessner House (6) (tours, 312-326-1480). Kitty-corner to the Glessner House, on the northeast corner of 18th and Prairie, is the site of the now-demolished Pullman Mansion. It's also said to be the site of the Fort Dearborn Massacre. A half block south on Prairie, the mansion built for Marshall Field Jr. in 1884 still stands at 1919 S. Prairie. It was recently divided into condominiums.

a large city would be built up there," he later commented.

"At this period," Fonda continued, "Chicago was merely an Indian Agency; it contained about 14 homes, and not more than 75 to 100 inhabitants at the most. An agent of the American Fur Company, named Gurdon S. Hubbard, then occupied the fort. The staple business seemed to be carried on by Indians and run-away soldiers, who hunted ducks and muskrats in the marshes. There was a great deal of low land, and mostly destitute of timber."

Another image of what life was like in 1820s Chicago was described in a letter

Brothers in Arms

A NUMBER OF SOLDIERS who would later fight against each other in the U.S. Civil War (1861–65) fought side by side in defense of their country in the Black Hawk War. In addition to Union General Winfield Scott, other officers included Jefferson Davis (future president of the Confederate States) and Nathan Boone (son of Daniel Boone). Abraham Lincoln served in the Illinois militia at the time, but he did not fight on the battlefield.

written by early settler Alexander Wolcott to his brother-in-law living on the East Coast.

The principal part of my stock consists in two horses, ten milk cows (two yoke of oxen belonging to Uncle Sam) and about ten head of young cattle. Mr. Kinzie planted for me during my absence six acres of corn from which I gathered three hundred and seventy measured bushels, more than sixty bushels to the acre, a pretty good crop that, considering the season. I intend next spring to enclose a pasture of about a hundred acres to keep my cows and twenty sheep. . . . During the winter and spring I propose to build an additional kitchen, a store-house, a blacksmith's shop, a council house, and office, an old fashioned Connecticut corn-barn, a poultry house, a smoke-house, a milk-house, and a root-house, besides putting up enclosure of palings around my yard etc. Do you see I do not propose to be idle between this and the next planting season? If Uncle Sam lets me stay on this farm of his for five of six years I intend to make it one of the most convenient and inviting little posts in the country.

THE NATIVES' LAST STAND

As more and more white settlers like Wolcott moved into the area, the Native

Schoolcraft's sketch of Chicago as it appeared in 1820. Kinzie's home is on the right, and the rebuilt Fort Dearborn is on the left.
COURTESY OF KENAN HEISE

Americans made one last effort to hold onto their territory. In April 1832 the Sauk warrior Black Hawk led 1,000 warriors into the Great Lakes region to reclaim their lands. Fort Dearborn received reinforcements, and a force of 850 U.S. soldiers was assembled under the leadership of General Winfield Scott to meet the Sauk in battle. By September, all but 150 of Black Hawk's warriors were dead. Now safe from any major threat posed by Native Americans, Chicago became a magnet for settlers and speculators. From 1830 to 1840 the population increased from several hundred to almost 4,500.

Black Hawk (1767–1838).
THE NEWBERRY LIBRARY

4

From Small Town to Big City

IN THE 160 YEARS from the Europeans' arrival in 1673 to 1833, warfare, disease, and economic dependence took their toll on the Native American populations in the Great Lakes region. With Black Hawk's defeat, the only thing left to do was to make it official.

So it was in September 1833 that the United Bands of Chippewa, Ottawa, and Potawatomi Indians—about 6,000 in all—gathered in Chicago to sign over their final claims to all areas in Illinois and Chicago. The Native Americans "sold" approximately five million acres of Illinois land for a half million dollars in cash and another half million to be paid within two years. In 1835 the

Crews raising the grade of buildings on Chicago's Lake Street, 1857.

CHICAGO HISTORY MUSEUM, ICHI-00698

Time Line

1833	Treaty of Chicago: Native Americans sell land in Illinois and Wisconsin and move to reservation lands; Chicago incorporates as a town
1834	First drawbridges built to span Chicago River; Chicago River/Lake Michigan harbor and access improved
1837	Chicago incorporates as a city
1840	Chicago Anti-Slavery Society established
1845	Irish Potato Famine begins; millions of Irish emigrate to the United States, tens of thousands ending up in Chicago
1848	Telegraph service connects Chicago and eastern cities; I & M Canal completed; first Chicago railroads open
1856	Chicago Historical Society established
1857	Second Fort Dearborn demolished
1858	Abraham Lincoln and Stephen A. Douglas debate for Illinois Senate seat
1860	Republicans nominate Abraham Lincoln for U.S. President in Chicago's first national political convention
1861	Civil War begins
1862	Race riots in Chicago
1863	Emancipation Proclamation signed
1865	Civil War ends; Abraham Lincoln assassinated

"We have no sympathy with the morbid sentiment that would permit an insignificant number of worthless savages, incapable, as a whole of civilization, to stand in the way of development; and if we had, it would amount to nothing, for the weaker must succumb to the stronger."

—*CHICAGO AND ITS DISTINGUISHED CITIZENS*, 1881

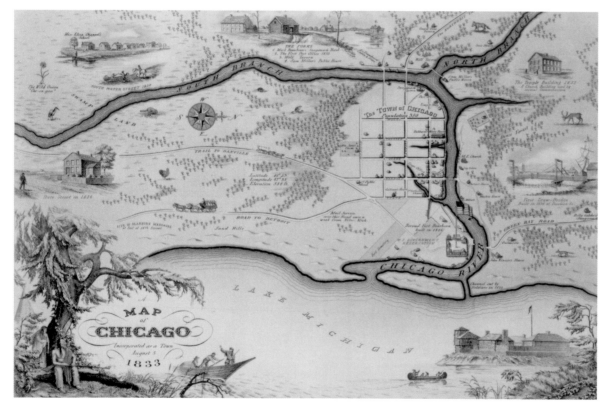

Chicago in 1833.

Potawatomi returned to Chicago to claim their final payments before relocating to reservations west of the Mississippi River.

This may sound like a lot of money, but what amount of money could ever make up for the loss of one's land and for the destruction of an entire way of life? In addition, the Native Americans never saw much of the money promised to them. Before making payments to the Indians, the U.S. government deducted large sums of money to pay off debts owed to white traders. The Kinzie family alone was paid $42,000. Another $17,000 went to the American Fur Company.

But what choice did the Native Americans really have?

The U.S. government wouldn't negotiate directly with the tribal elders. Instead, they worked out an agreement with two men of mixed American Indian and European ancestry, Billy Caldwell and Alexander Robinson. Caldwell and Robinson were sympathetic with the Americans. Earlier, they helped to keep the Potawatomi from joining forces with Black Hawk. The U.S. government rewarded Caldwell and Robinson with large pieces of property in the area, as well as annual payments for the remainder of their lives. The rest of the tribes didn't fare so well.

Potawatomi Chief Shabbona (1775–1859) was one of the signers of the 1833 Treaty of Chicago.
COURTESY OF KENAN HEISE

Outnumbered, outgunned, and now outdone at the negotiating table, the Native Americans were given two years to leave the area. In the meantime they traded much of their treaty money for trade goods, leaving few assets by the time their final departure date arrived in 1835. Their last act of protest was to perform a threatening war dance throughout the city of Chicago on the day

they arrived to claim their final payment. One resident at the time, John Caton, witnessed the frightening scene firsthand:

> They assembled at the council-house, where the Lake House now stands, on the north side of the river. All were entirely naked, except a strip of cloth around the loins. Their bodies were covered all over with a great variety of brilliant paints. . . . The long, coarse, black hair was gathered into scalp locks on the top of their heads, and decorated with a profusion of hawk's and eagle's feathers. . . . Their eyes were wild and blood-shot. Their countenances had assumed an expression of terrible hate, dire revenge, remorseless cruelty. . . . Their muscles stood out in great hard knots, as if wrought to a tension which must burst them. Their tomahawks were thrown and brandished about in every direction, with the most terrible ferocity, and with a force and energy which could only result from the highest excitement, and with every step and every gesture they uttered the most frightful yells. . . . It seemed as if we had a picture of hell itself before us. . . . What if they should, in their maddened frenzy, turn this sham warfare into a real attack? How easy it would be for them to massacre us all, and leave not a living soul to tell the story. . . . I think all felt relieved when the last had disappeared around the corner as they

Champion of the Dispossessed

CHICAGO WRITER Nelson Algren (1909–1981) was the ultimate friend of the little guy. His works celebrated Chicagoans who were short on luck and long on hard times. In his prose poem *Chicago: City on the Make*, Algren traced the corruption and greed he witnessed in Chicago in the mid-1900s all the way back to the founding of the city. After all, how different were the "Pottawattomies" from the hungry kids and underpaid, overworked laborers of Algren's time?

The term Algren used to describe those who had power and used it selfishly was "hustlers." By that he meant anyone who was "out to make a fast buck off whoever was standing nearest." The city's early hustlers "paid the Pottawottomies off in cash in the cool of the Indian evening: and had the cash back to the dime by the break of the Indian dawn." Algren's poetic history of Chicago could have been dedicated to anyone who was ever hustled in the city on the make.

passed down Lake Street. . . . From thence they passed down to Fort Dearborn, concluding their performance in the presence of the officers and soldiers of the garrison. . . .

CHICAGO'S DAWNING

With the Native Americans removed from their homeland, the floodgates were now wide open to white settlement and urban progress. In 1833 Chicago was officially

Second City Firsts (1833)

First official code of laws passed

First jail built (Clark and Randolph)

First newspaper, the *Chicago Democrat,* published

First Chicago brewery opens for business

First brickyard, brick house, and lumberyard open for business

First public school opens, with Eliza Chappell as teacher

First slaughterhouse opens, and first shipments of pork from Chicago to eastern markets

incorporated as a town. Four years later it achieved its status as a full-fledged city. The new but rapidly growing city was showing the first signs of its future importance, especially in terms of trade and as a transportation center. A traveler and businessman returning to Chicago in 1833 described it as "an Indian wigwam town changed into an American city in the course of three or four years."

Where there had only been about 10 or so buildings three years before, another 1833 visitor estimated, "I believe there has been a hundred built this year, all without any regard to beauty, and they are set on blocks so that they can move them at the shortest notice." Living in these buildings were people from all different backgrounds and parts of the world. This fact was noticed by another visitor to the new city, who observed, "the inhabitants are a singular collection of beings . . . black and white and red and grey, and they live in all manner of ways." From the very beginning, it seems, Chicago has been a multicultural city.

Equally surprised by the diversity of this new city, if less impressed, an easterner named Charles J. Latrobe said of Chicago, "the village and its occupants presented a most motley scene. . . . You will find horse-dealers and horse stealers—rogues

Gurdon S. Hubbard (1802–1886).
HISTORY OF CHICAGO, A. T. ANDREAS COMPANY, 1884–86

of every description—white, black, brown, and red; half-breeds, quarter-breeds, and men of no breed at all; dealers in pigs, poultry, and potatoes."

Latrobe described the central area of the "village" as a "chaos of mud, rubbish, and confusion." Latrobe was no more complimentary about Chicago's early architecture. "Frame and clapboard houses were springing up daily under the active axes and hammers of the speculators, and piles of lumber announced preparation for yet other edifices of an equally light character." Witnessing all this, Latrobe concluded that "all was in such a state of most appalling confusion, filth, and racket."

Chicago officially went from being a town to a city in 1837, but it would take more than a document to change Chicago from a little prairie town to a full-blown city. It would take the Illinois & Michigan Canal, improved farming technology, and a lot more people. The Erie Canal opened in 1825, connecting the Great Lakes with the eastern markets. The Illinois & Michigan Canal would extend the all-water passage to the Mississippi River, with Chicago as a key midpoint between agricultural products like corn, beans, and meat moving east and manufactured goods like furniture, cookware, and clothing moving west. As the final link connecting Lake Michigan to the Gulf of Mexico, the canal also connected north and south, which made it easier and more economical to transport, for example, Wisconsin and Michigan lumber to new and growing towns in southern Illinois and beyond.

Chicago's transformation—like that of a caterpillar to a butterfly—was in progress, but not everyone saw it coming. Mark Beaubien, the easygoing French-Canadian owner of Chicago's first hotel, gave away parcels of land in hopes that more people would settle there. It wasn't long before the people who received Beaubien's gifts turned around and sold them for large amounts of money. It didn't bother Beaubien much. "Didn't expect no town," he said.

Two of the early speculators who did see the potential value in Chicago were Gurdon S. Hubbard and William B. Ogden. Hubbard, unlike John Kinzie, was one of the former Indian traders to make a successful transition from a fur-based economy to a land-based economy. In addition to real estate, Hubbard also did business in meatpacking, warehousing, banking, and insurance.

Ogden was even more successful than Hubbard. A former easterner, Ogden made his first trip to Chicago to survey some land purchased by his brother-in-law. His first impressions of the town were dismal. After looking over the waterlogged parcel of land he wrote his brother-in-law that he had "been guilty of an act of great folly in making [this] purchase." Ogden recommended that his brother-in-law unload what he considered worthless properties. To his surprise, the properties quickly sold for still higher prices.

Ogden changed his mind about Chicago, and changed his plans to move back east. A year later, the lawyer and former New York state legislator was elected Chicago's first mayor. John H. Kinzie, son of John Kinzie, came in second place in votes.

Hubbard and Ogden both realized that Chicago's future lay in its location as a trading center between east and west. So it's not surprising that they were both instrumental in getting the Illinois & Michigan Canal built. The first shovelful of dirt was dug on July 4, 1836. Because of

William B. Ogden (1805–1877), Chicago's first mayor.
COURTESY OF KENAN HEISE

financial problems, it took 12 years before the first barge traffic used the new canal. Transportation of goods skyrocketed after the canal was complete. By 1850, the population of Chicago approached 30,000, with almost 125,000 citizens residing in the surrounding counties.

Who were all these newcomers? Where would they all live? And what kinds of jobs could they find? The construction of the canal itself required many new workers, many of whom were poor immigrants who fled starvation brought on by the potato famine in Ireland. Large numbers of Chicago immigrants also came from Germany, Great Britain, and Sweden.

People were also hard at work building homes and businesses, working in the ports and warehouses, in meatpacking slaughter-houses, and in factories making clothing. Iron and steel became major industries in the 1850s, especially after the railroad industry took off. As a result of the great numbers of people moving to Chicago from the east and from other countries, there was plenty of cheap labor to forge the rails that would connect Chicago to the east and west. Chicago was now well on its way to becoming a major urban center.

Two new innovations played a big role in transforming Chicago into a major trading

Remarkably, this house built in 1836 is still standing. The Clarke House is currently owned by the city of Chicago and is open for tours.
CLARKE HOUSE MUSEUM

center: the reaper and the railroads. Neither one of them was invented or first developed in Chicago, but each one made a huge impact on the city's growth and importance.

STACKER OF WHEAT, PLAYER WITH RAILROADS

Before farming machines were invented, wheat was harvested by hand using a scythe or sickle—a long, curved blade attached to the end of a wooden handle. Using this method, the average farmer could hope to grow and harvest enough wheat for his family, with maybe a little left over to sell.

This all changed when the son of a farmer, Cyrus Hall McCormick, invented a machine that could do the work of 20 men. McCormick received a patent for his "Virginia Reaper" in 1834, but he didn't make or sell very many until after he moved to Chicago in 1848. William Ogden persuaded McCormick that Chicago would be the perfect place to manufacture and sell his reapers.

McCormick's invention was the right idea at the right time. And Chicago was the ideal place for a young enterprising man to make his fortune. By 1850 the McCormick Reaper Works was churning out high-quality reaper machines. But these machines were expensive. Farming the old-fashioned way, it would have taken farmers years to save up enough money to purchase one of McCormick's reapers. This is where McCormick's other major innovation came in. He sold his reapers on credit. That is, he delivered his product to his customers up front, in exchange for a down payment and the promise to make regular payments toward the balance. This way, farmers could use the new machinery before they could afford to buy it.

The "Virginia Reaper" obviously helped individual farmers. It also had a big impact on grain markets. Wheat grain was now pouring into Chicago by the tons, transported on newly laid train tracks as well as the recently opened Illinois & Michigan Canal. This created whole new industries in Chicago and revolutionized old ones. The Chicago Board of Trade helped stabilize grain markets by setting standards for different grades of grain, making Chicago the preferred place for farmers to sell and merchants to buy wheat. Wheat was measured and divided in grain elevators, stored in warehouses, and shipped by train and by boat.

The development of railroad lines in the United States made it much easier and more economical to move the harvested grain (and other farming products) from the farms out west to the markets out east. It also eased the movement of products from east to west. Chicago was the focal point of the railway system, like the hub of a wheel, in which all the spokes radiate outward from the city.

NEWCOMERS TO A NEW CITY

The new jobs created by the transportation, manufacturing, and warehousing industries meant even more people were moving to Chicago. Some new arrivals were easterners: second and third sons who saw their family farms handed down to the first son; investors drawn by skyrocketing land values, which meant they could make a lot of money buying and selling land; inventors who saw opportunities to be had in a changing economy. Others immigrated to Chicago from foreign lands: Ireland, England, Germany, Italy, Sweden, Lithuania, Serbia, Croatia, Poland, even China, Japan, and Russia.

The Pioneer was the first locomotive to pull a train on Chicago's new rail system, in 1848.
COURTESY OF KENAN HEISE

37

John Wentworth (1815–1888).

HISTORY OF CHICAGO, A. T. ANDREAS COMPANY, 1884–86

This initial wave of foreign immigrants helped Chicago grow quickly. It also ensured that Chicago would be a melting pot of ethnic groups.

Among the newcomers to Chicago was John Wentworth, a grandson of one of the signers of the Articles of Confederation. Wentworth probably looked more like a farmhand when he ambled into town in 1836, barefoot and mud-splattered. It's not that Wentworth didn't have any boots. It's just that he carried them on his journey west so that they'd be clean when he arrived in Chicago for the job interviews he hoped to get. The young graduate of Dartmouth College also carried with him a letter of introduction from Isaac Hill, governor of New Hampshire and a friend of the Wentworth family. In part the letter said, "Mr. Wentworth possesses merit as a scholar and a gentleman, and has already discovered talent as a politician which gives him the first rank among our young men. He goes to the West in pursuit of fortune and fame."

He found both, pretty much in that order. Within one month, Wentworth became editor of the *Chicago Democrat* newspaper. Three years later he bought the newspaper, serving as editor and publisher. The newspaper provided Wentworth with a pulpit from which he preached his unique brand of Democratic politics. This became a great advantage when Wentworth later ran for mayor, a job he won and held from 1857 to 1858 and again from 1860 to 1861.

At six feet, six inches tall and upward of 300 pounds, "Long" John Wentworth was an intimidating figure who was used to getting his way. He once delivered what Carl Sandburg later described as "the shortest and most terrifying stump speech ever heard in Illinois." Addressing a rowdy crowd, he bellowed, "You damn fools. . . . You can either vote for me or you can go to hell."

Wentworth's informal nature also produced one of the most famous quotes to come out of the young city. When the Prince of Wales visited the city, Wentworth introduced him this way to a crowd gathered beneath the Tremont Hotel balcony: "Boys, this is the prince. Prince, these are the boys."

Before he died in 1888, Wentworth designed his own monumental grave marker at Rosehill Cemetery, a 72-foot-high obelisk, as oversized and imposing as his personality and influence.

1800s Population Explosion

YEAR	CHICAGO POPULATION
1833	150–200
1840	4,470
1850	29,963
1860	112,172
1870	298,977

WOODEN CITY

As more and more newcomers moved west, Chicago experienced its first major building boom in the 1850s. Using new technologies, sawmills in Wisconsin and Michigan could cheaply cut trees into uniform-sized boards (instead of irregularly sized and shaped logs, notched out at the ends to fit together like huge Lincoln Logs). Much of this lumber arrived in Chicago by boat, via Lake Michigan. Wood not used to build up the rapidly growing city of Chicago was transported south via the I&M Canal or east and west via railroad.

Despite advances in technology, many of the buildings of this era were still relatively simple in design. Using "balloon frame" architecture (so named because critics said the slightest breeze could blow them away), Chicago was quickly populated by two-story wood frame buildings. Wood-plank sidewalks and streets were built to help the growing numbers of pedestrians and horse-drawn wagons navigate Chicago's muddy ground.

PUBLIC WORKS

The massive increase in city population caused major problems in terms of public health. Today people take clean drinking water and indoor plumbing for granted. Most Americans don't think twice before filling a glass of water, taking a shower, or flushing a toilet. Back then it was a lot different. For one thing there were no underground sewers, and very few buildings had indoor plumbing. This meant that human waste and other refuse ran in open gutters along the streets. Imagine the odors—and the potential for disease.

MUDHOLE OF THE PRAIRIE

Before it was known as the Second City, the Windy City, or the City of Big Shoulders, Chicago was often called the Mudhole of the Prairie. For good reason. The city was prone to flooding, especially in the spring, making the streets so muddy that people, horses, and carts frequently got stuck.

An old joke that was popular at the time went something like this: A man is stuck up to his waist in a muddy Chicago street. Asked if he needs help, he replies, "No thanks, I've got a good horse under me."

But, as one visitor to the city noted, the soggy streets were no laughing matter. "Under these planks the water was standing on the surface over three-fourths of the city, and as the sewers from the houses were emptied under them, a frightful odor was

Name Game

BEFORE IT WAS KNOWN as the Mudhole of the Prairie, Chicago was often referred to as the Garden City. In fact, Chicago's official motto, adopted in 1837, is *Urbs in Horto*, which is Latin for "city in a garden."

Everybody knows that Chicago is often called the Windy City, but few agree on why. It's true that the strong and often cold wind off Lake Michigan could have been the inspiration for the nickname; others argue that people from other cities often used the nickname to poke fun at Chicagoans' long-winded boasts about their city.

Chicago became known as the Second City after it outgrew Philadelphia in 1890. Chicagoans show no signs of giving up the title, even if Los Angeles recently surpassed Chicago's population.

Several of the city's most famous nicknames came from Carl Sandburg's poem "Chicago" (1916). From it, we get Hog Butcher for the World and City of the Big Shoulders. Thanks to Nelson Algren, the city is also called the City on the Make. And the first Mayor Daley was fond of calling Chicago the City That Works.

Water on the Brain

GUESS WHO DESIGNED the system for turning Lake Michigan water into the city's drinking water? None other than Ellis Chesbrough. It all starts with those water intakes (called cribs) that sit several miles off the city's lakeshore. One crew started digging at the crib and one started digging on shore. At a depth of about 60 feet, the two crews met somewhere in the middle. Amazingly, they were only about one inch off-center.

emitted in summer causing fevers and other diseases. . . . This was notably the case during the summer of 1854 when the cholera visited the place destroying the population at the rate of one hundred and fifty a day."

The city planners decided to build an underground sewage system, but there was a problem. There simply wasn't enough difference between the height of the ground level and the water level. Waste water can't drain unless pipes are pitched at an angle. The only two options were to lower the Chicago River or raise the city.

An engineer named Ellis Chesbrough convinced the city that it had no choice but to build the sewers above ground and then cover them with dirt. This raised the level of the city's streets by as much as 12 feet.

This of course created a new problem: huge mounds of dirt practically buried the first floors of every building in Chicago.

Building owners were faced with a choice: either convert the first floors of their buildings into basements, and the second stories into main floors, or raise the entire buildings to meet the new street level. Small wood-frame buildings could be lifted fairly easily. But what about large, heavy structures like the Tremont Hotel, which was a six-story brick building?

That's where George Mortimer Pullman came in. He had already established a successful house-moving business in Albion, New York. After arriving in Chicago, he and his brother Albert applied their skills to many of the city's larger structures. To hoist a big structure like the Tremont Hotel, Pullman would place thousands of jackscrews beneath the building's foundation. One man was assigned to operate each section of roughly 10 jack-screws. At Pullman's signal each man turned

This detail of "Major Watersheds of Illinois" shows the dividing line of the Chicago region's watersheds.

SALLY A. MCCONKEY AND KATHLEEN J. BROWN, ILLINOIS STATE WATER SURVEY, ILLINOIS DEPARTMENT OF NATURAL RESOURCES, JANUARY 2002

Re-create the Chicago River Watershed

River waters come from many different sources, including natural springs, lakes, other rivers and streams, as well as run-off rain water. The surrounding land that feeds rainwater toward a body of water is called a watershed. Water always travels downhill, so the rain that feeds the Chicago River falls on ground that resides within the Chicago River watershed.

The Chicago River watershed extends about 80 miles from north (near Gurnee, Illinois) to south (near Beecher, Illinois). A narrow strip of land close to the Lake Michigan shoreline belongs to the Lake Michigan watershed. Rain that falls on the east side of the ridges created by glacial moraines tens of thousands of years ago flows down into Lake Michigan. The rain that falls on the west side of these high points feeds the Chicago River, as well as the Calumet River to the south of downtown Chicago. The western border of the Chicago River watershed is formed by a continental divide. Rain that falls just west of this divide feeds the Des Plaines River.

Using the materials below, re-create a clay model version of the Chicago River and its watershed.

YOU'LL NEED

1 package of white modeling clay
9 x 13-inch disposable aluminum pan
plastic butter knife
spray bottle
water
blue food coloring

Flatten the modeling clay and spread it out on the bottom of the aluminum pan. Using the watershed map as your guide, cut out the Lake Michigan shoreline with the plastic knife and remove the excess clay. Then carve the approximate shape of the Chicago and Des Plaines Rivers.

Make two clay snakes, one 13 inches long and one 8 inches long. Place the longer snake approximately where the western edge of the Chicago River watershed belongs, and the shorter snake where the eastern edge belongs. Flatten the snakes slightly with your fingers.

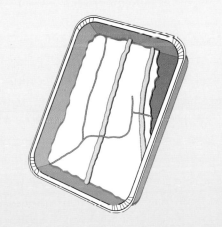

Fill the spray bottle with water and a few drops of blue food coloring so that it's easier to see which direction the water flows. Re-create a rainstorm by spraying the clay watershed. With each spray you'll see water beads fall to one side or another of the ridges.

The water should travel downward and collect in the river you carved in the clay. If it doesn't, you can pour the water out and change the height of the clay landscape before trying again.

This activity was developed with assistance from the Friends of the Chicago River (www.chicagoriver.org.), a nonprofit organization dedicated to fostering the vitality of the Chicago River for the plant, animal, and human communities within its watershed.

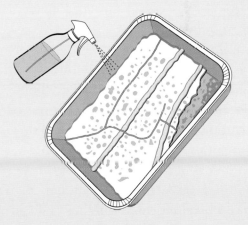

41

Bubbly Creek

BEGINNING IN the late 1860s, the meatpacking plants along the Chicago River were one of the waterway's biggest polluters, dumping unwanted animal parts into the south fork of the river. The decaying remnants of hogs and cows released gases that bubbled up to the surface. In a letter to his brother Cyrus, William McCormick once wrote, "The river is positively red with blood under the Rush Street bridge and down past our factory! What a pestilence may result from it I don't know." At times a solid crust of grease would form on the surface of the river, enabling wild chickens to actually walk on water.

his jackscrew the same amount at the same time, thereby raising the building slowly and evenly. Astonishingly, the Tremont Hotel stayed open during the entire operation, and many of its guests didn't even notice anything was happening.

Pullman made a small fortune lifting buildings. He later used his money to make a bigger fortune building Pullman sleeper cars, which were luxurious train accommodations for wealthy travelers.

Some people like to say that every problem has a solution. But in Chicago's early history, every engineering solution seemed to create a new problem. Now that Chicago's wastewater was draining efficiently into the Chicago River, the already polluted river basically became an open sewer. One visitor in the mid-1800s called the Chicago River "a sluggish, slimy stream, too lazy to clean itself."

The worst part was that the polluted river flowed into Lake Michigan, which was Chicago's source for drinking water. Now what? If the city had proven that it could lift itself higher, then it could certainly make nature bend to its will. Ellis Chesbrough, the engineer who convinced the city to raise its buildings, now suggested that the city reverse the direction of the river's flow so that all the contaminated water would flow away from Lake Michigan. To pull off this engineering stunt, Chesbrough again relied on the laws of gravity.

The Chicago River had been connected to the Illinois & Michigan Canal since 1848. In 1871 Chesbrough directed crews to deepen the Illinois & Michigan Canal. Then, using pumps, he redirected the flow of the river southwest toward the Illinois River, which runs into the Mississippi River. This pulled the current away from Lake Michigan. However, the current was never completely and permanently reversed until the Chicago River was connected to the Chicago Sanitary and Ship Canal in 1900. Ever since, Chicago's water pollution has become the problem of cities downstream.

With its sanitation problems solved, Chicago took another step toward becoming a major American city. The next step was facilitated by the city's role in fighting the Civil War.

THE SPOILS OF WAR

Although the battlefronts were hundreds of miles from Chicago, the Civil War had profound impacts on Chicago's citizens, industries, and civic institutions. Before the war, Chicago was running behind St. Louis, Missouri, and Cincinnati, Ohio, in the race for economic leadership in the Midwest. St. Louis led the country in grain distribution, and Cincinnati was the nation's meatpacking capital. But both of those cities were farther south than Chicago and therefore closer to the frontlines of the Civil War. Shipments of grain on the Mississippi River and meat products on the Ohio River were vulnerable to rebel attacks.

As the central hub of the northern railroad system Chicago could safely transport its goods throughout the Civil War. As a result, Chicago got a lot of war-time business that might have otherwise gone to St. Louis and Cincinnati. In this way the war actually helped Chicago emerge as the new frontrunner in these important industries. The growing meat-packing industry eventually led to the opening of the Union Stockyards in 1865. From that time until the 1920s Chicago was the world leader in the butchering and distribution of pork and beef.

The distance from the battlefront also made Chicago an ideal place to manufacture uniforms, guns, and ammunition. With all these new sources of trade, Chicago's

The Republican Party held its 1860 convention at the Wigwam building in Chicago. Illinois delegates packed the convention house with rowdy supporters of Abraham Lincoln, who nominated the Springfield lawyer as their candidate for the presidential election.

Camp Douglas

DURING THE CIVIL WAR, Chicago was the site of a massive prisoner-of-war camp named after Stephen A. Douglas, the senator of Illinois who was famous for his debates with Abraham Lincoln. The camp, situated on land owned by Douglas on the southern edge of the city, started out as a training center for newly enlisted Chicago soldiers. Later, captured Confederate soldiers were imprisoned at Camp Douglas. Poor living conditions led to outbreaks of disease and malnutrition. Over the course of the war, more than 25,000 rebel soldiers were incarcerated at Camp Douglas, and more than 4,000 died there.

economy grew much faster than it would have without the war.

Even though the cannon fire and battle cries could not be heard from Chicago, the twin tragedies of war and slavery brought the Civil War home to the city. Many Chicagoans eagerly enlisted to fight the Confederacy and fought bravely at battles like Chickamauga, Shiloh, and Gettysburg. Of approximately 15,000 soldiers from the Chicago area, nearly 4,000 never returned alive. Many more were injured.

Not all Chicagoans supported President Abraham Lincoln and the Union cause. "Copperhead" was the term for northerners who were opposed to fighting the Civil War in order to preserve the Union. The *Chicago Times* newspaper was so critical of President Lincoln that Union General Ambrose Burnside shut the newspaper down. Lincoln later reversed this decision.

The main reasons for opposition to the war were racism and competition for unskilled labor jobs. Poor foreign-born immigrants worried that freed slaves would move to Chicago and take their jobs because they'd be willing to work for lower wages. In 1862 these rising tensions erupted into a race riot in Chicago, pitting whites against free blacks.

Opponents of the Union cause were troublesome enough. Those who saw the war as an opportunity to profit presented additional problems. Some army suppliers charged overly high prices for the horses, wagons, guns, uniforms, and food they sold to the Union army. Another particularly nagging problem was desertion—soldiers who ran away from their regiments. Soldiers were routinely paid a bonus (called a bounty) for enlisting in the army. Many would sneak away from their regiments after they got

An early campaign poster shows a young, beardless Abraham Lincoln.
LIBRARY OF CONGRESS, LC-USZ62-92281

paid—only to re-enlist later to receive another bounty. Some especially dishonest individuals made a lot of money doing this over and over.

In *The Gem of the Prairie*, a book on the history of crime in Chicago, author Herbert Asbury describes the activities of a man aptly named Con Brown, "a horse-thief and all-around bad man" as well as "the prince of bounty-jumpers."

"During the first three years of the war," Asbury writes, "Con Brown got himself on the rolls of no fewer than twenty military

Next Stop, Freedom

DURING THE CIVIL WAR, Chicago was one of the stops on the Underground Railroad, the informal series of secret stopping points on an escaped slave's journey to freedom. A number of prominent Chicagoans participated in the efforts to transport African American slaves to freedom in the North, including John and Mary Jones and private detective Allan Pinkerton, as well as a variety of other civic and religious leaders.

How Free Was Free?

EVEN THOUGH CHICAGO was in the North, where there was no slavery, African Americans living there suffered many injustices. African Americans in Illinois were not permitted to vote. They weren't even allowed to live in the state without written proof that they were free. Any African American in Illinois found without certificates of freedom could be considered a runaway slave and thrown in prison. In some cases they could even be sold into slavery.

This actually happened once in Chicago. In 1842 a free African American named Edwin Heathcock was arrested. Because he didn't have a certificate of freedom, Heathcock was offered for sale at a public auction. Fortunately for Heathcock, the only bidder was an attorney named Mahlon Ogden, the younger brother of Chicago's first mayor, William B. Ogden. Once the public auction was complete, Ogden immediately announced to Heathcock, loud enough for the large surrounding crowd to hear, "I have given a quarter for you. You are my man, my slave! Now, then, go where you please! You are free."

Chicago African American John Jones's certificate of freedom.

CHICAGO HISTORY MUSEUM, ICHI-31975

These paintings are of John (1816–1879) and Mary (1819–1910) Jones, prominent African Americans who moved to Chicago in 1845. The Jones's tailor business must have been fairly successful if they were able to afford to hire a portrait artist. John Jones also wrote several articles and pamphlets to promote the abolition of slavery.

CHICAGO HISTORY MUSEUM, ICHI-10896, ICHI-10897, PAINTINGS BY AARON E. DARLING

Walking Tour: Rosehill Cemetery

(5800 N. Ravenswood Ave., Chicago, Illinois; 773-561-5940)

Call ahead for a schedule of free tours. You can also pay for a guided tour offered by the Chicago History Museum (www.chicagohistory.org) or the Chicago Architecture Foundation (www.architecture.org). When you get to the cemetery, be sure to request a map of the grounds.

Rosehill Cemetery is notable for the large number of Union Civil War soldiers buried there. Near the Ravenswood entrance by the grave site of General Thomas Ransom, you'll find a section with row after row of white headstones honoring Civil War soldiers. Another popular Civil War monument, the Rock of Chickamauga, honors General George H. Thomas, who led the Union forces in the Battle of Chickamauga. General Thomas is not buried near the massive boulder taken from the battleground site, but many veterans of the Civil War are.

Rosehill Cemetery is the final resting place for 18 Chicago mayors, including "Long" John Wentworth, Levi Boone (Daniel Boone's grand-nephew), Roswell B. Mason, George B. Swift, and Buckner Morris.

Several prominent business leaders are buried at Rosehill, including Oscar Mayer, Richard Warren Sears, John G. Shedd, A. Montgomery Ward, and Ignaz Schwinn (of bicycle fame). Other notable Chicagoans buried at Rosehill include Stephen A. Douglas, Wilbur Storey, Charles J. Hull, and Myra Bradwell.

The namesakes for four of Chicago's streets are on grave markers at Rosehill. See if you can find Hoyne, Kedzie, Peterson, and Wells.

The most unusual grave marker at Rosehill may belong to Lulu Fellows, a girl who died in 1883 at the age of 16. Her lifelike statue is encased in glass to protect it from rain and vandals.

A poster used to recruit Chicagoans to join the Union army during the Civil War.
COURTESY OF KENAN HEISE

organizations and collected about eight thousand dollars in bounties."

But these bounty-jumpers were the exception. Most soldiers served the Union army with bravery and dedication. It was not uncommon for groups of young Chicagoans to organize their own companies of volunteers, such as the 2nd Chicago Board of Trade Regiment, the Railroad Regiment, and Irish Legion. What these amateur soldiers lacked in training they made up for in courage and their belief in the righteousness of their cause.

Elmer E. Ellsworth's Chicago Zouave Cadets.

One of the city's most celebrated groups of volunteers was Ellsworth's Chicago Zouaves Cadets. The regiment was named after Elmer E. Ellsworth, a young officer who had previously worked at Abraham Lincoln's law office. The Zouave Cadets wore colorful uniforms and were famous for performing well-coordinated military drills.

It turns out that Ellsworth would be the first Union officer killed in the Civil War. When informed of Ellsworth's death, President Lincoln broke down in tears. "I will make no apology . . . for my weakness," Lincoln said, because "I knew poor Elmer Ellsworth well and held him in great regard."

The first African Americans to enlist were actually turned away by the state of Illinois, and were forced to enlist with the 54th Massachusetts Colored Infantry. Later in the war Chicago had its own regiment of African American soldiers, the 29th Regiment of U.S. Colored Infantry, commanded by Chicagoan John Bross.

Of course, everyone knows the outcome of the Civil War: the Emancipation Proclamation and the victory of the Union forces, followed by Lincoln's assassination.

The final act in that national drama is symbolized for Chicagoans in Lincoln's funeral service held on May 1, 1865. The President's body lay in state in Chicago's courthouse at Randolph and Clark, just six blocks from the Wigwam building where he had been nominated to run for president almost exactly five years earlier. It's estimated that 120,000 Chicagoans paid their respects to Lincoln.

Chicagoans gather to pay their final respects to President Abraham Lincoln. Lincoln's casket was on view at the Chicago Courthouse before heading to Springfield, Illinois, for burial.

5

Reduced to Ashes

BY 1870 CHICAGO HAD BECOME a true metropolis. In the previous decade, the number of people living in Chicago had tripled, from about 100,000 in 1860 to nearly 300,000 in 1870. Even more astounding, there were 10 times as many Chicagoans in 1870 as there were in 1850, when the population was less than 30,000.

Chicago's economy had also grown enormously since 1850, when the city's fortunes were just beginning to benefit from its new transportation network of rail lines and canals. Reading *A Guide to the City of Chicago*, published in 1868, a visitor to Chicago would learn that Chicago had taken the lead in the lumber trade.

Chicago in 1868, just three years before the Great Fire.
LIBRARY OF CONGRESS, LC-USZC2 2092

Time Line

October 7, 1871	Fire breaks out at a lumber mill on the Near West Side of Chicago
October 8	
Morning	The October 7 fire is extinguished; three tons of hay delivered to O'Leary barn
7:30–8:00 P.M.	O'Leary family retires for the night
8:45 P.M.	O'Leary's neighbor notices fire in O'Leary barn
10:30 P.M.	Fire officially reported as "out of control"
11:30 P.M.	Fire jumps south fork of Chicago River
October 9	
1:30 A.M.	State Street bridge catches fire
2:30 A.M.	Courthouse bell crashes to floor; fire jumps main branch of the Chicago River
11:00 P.M.	Fire approaches Fullerton Avenue; light rain begins to fall
October 10	
3:00 A.M.	Rain strengthens, extinguishing the fire

Hog Butcher for the World,
Tool Maker, Stacker of Wheat,
Player with Railroads and the
Nation's Freight Handler;
Stormy, husky, brawling,
City of the Big Shoulders

—FROM THE POEM "CHICAGO" (1916)
BY CARL SANDBURG

"Like the grain and cattle trade, it has developed itself into startling proportions. From thirty-three millions of feet [of lumber] received in Chicago, in 1847, it has increased until it reached, in 1867, the amount of *seven hundred ninety-five millions of feet.*"

The authors of the 1868 guide recognized that Chicago was undergoing major changes and growth. Up until recently, they said, Chicago had been little more than the place where goods passed through on their way to other markets. "It was a buyer and seller on a grand scale; but it made scarcely anything, depending on the Eastern States for supplies of manufactured merchandise."

By 1868 that had all changed. "At the present time, almost every article of much bulk used upon railroads, in farming, in

The owners of Crosby's Opera House had just completed extensive remodeling of this magnificent building. The first performance was scheduled to take place on October 9, 1871. But the opera house burned down before the opening curtain ever went up.

CHICAGO HISTORY MUSEUM, ICHI-18413

warming houses, in building houses, or in cooking, is made in Chicago. Four thousand persons are engaged in manufacturing boots and shoes. Pianos . . . are also made on a great scale in the city." Of course, Chicago was also home to the McCormick Reaper Works, which employed hundreds in the manufacture of agricultural machinery.

Chicago was making more money and attracting more citizens, but it was also the scene of a cultural flowering. Ignoring the drawbacks complained about by many visitors to the city—like the filthy air, howling noises, and foul odors created by factories, steam engines, and sewage—the authors of the guide boasted of the city's

Play Ball

ON MAY 8, 1871, Chicago's first professional baseball team, the Chicago White Stockings, took the field in its first game against the Cleveland Forest Citys. The White Stockings won that game by a score of 14–12. They went on to take second place that year, but then had to take the next two years off because the Great Chicago Fire destroyed their ballpark and equipment.

wonders and beauties: its grand hotels, theaters, and opera houses; its lakefront, parks, and boulevards.

Perhaps the guidebook authors went too far in bragging about the city's "Nicholson Pavement," a style of street construction unique to Chicago: "It is considered far superior and more durable and economical than stone, which is so popular in other cities." But because it was made of wood and coal tar, it was also a lot more flammable than streets in other cities.

THE NOT-AS-GREAT FIRE

October 7, 1871. A fire starts in a wood-cutting mill on the West Side of Chicago. No big deal. Fires were an everyday occurrence back then and usually nothing to worry about—unless *your* property was the one in flames. Besides, Chicago had one of the nation's best big-city fire departments, with a top-notch detection and response system. The department had successfully put out 700 fires in the previous year. Officials were not concerned.

In 1871 Chicagoans were in the middle of the worst drought they could remember. In the first week of October, the fire department had already battled the flames of 28 major fires—twice the average. So it was an

overworked and weary fire department that responded to the fire bells that Saturday night. The fire spread steadily, consuming a total of four city blocks (bound by the Chicago River on the east, Clinton Street on the west, Van Buren Street on the south, and Adams Street on the north) before it was finally contained the next morning.

But the next day's newspapers warned citizens that the city might not be so lucky in the future. The *Chicago Tribune* said, "For day's past, alarm has followed alarm, but the comparatively trifling losses have familiarized us to the pealing of the Court-house bell, and we had forgotten that the absence of rain for three weeks had left everything in so dry and inflammable a condition that a spark might set a fire which could sweep from end to end of the city." That spark would come sooner than anyone could have predicted.

A CITY CATCHES FIRE

H. W. S. Cleveland, a landscape architect living in Chicago, later recalled that on October 8, 1871, he had retrieved a copy of the *Chicago Tribune* during a walk he took to survey the damage caused by the previous day's fire. "At breakfast we were discussing it as a terrible calamity, little dreaming how soon it would sink into insignificance in comparison with the destruction which followed."

It's intriguing to wonder which Chicagoans read this news story and what their reactions may have been. Was it read by William B. Ogden, the first mayor of Chicago and by 1871 an aging millionaire with huge investments in Chicago? By rising capitalist Potter Palmer, who owned the year-old "fireproof" Palmer House Hotel as well as most of the store-fronts on State Street? By John B. Drake, owner of the world-famous Tremont House hotel? Or by Albert Crosby, who was busily preparing for the grand re-opening of the stunningly remodeled Crosby's Opera House—an event that never occurred?

Two people who were most likely too busy to read the papers were Patrick and Catherine O'Leary, Irish immigrants who

In 1871 the Chicago Fire Department had 193 fire fighters and 23 others working as lookouts, telegraph operators, and administrators. It had 16 companies using steam engines, like the "R. A. Williams" No. 17 pictured here, four companies equipped with hook-and-ladder vehicles, and six hose carts.

CHICAGO HISTORY MUSEUM, ICHI-31916

lived eight blocks south of the previous day's fire. Patrick O'Leary was a laborer and Catherine took care of their five kids as well as the five cows, one calf, and one horse living in their barn. Even though this was the city, many people still kept farm animals to supply food or provide additional sources of income. The industrious Mrs. O'Leary made a little extra money by selling the milk from their cows to her neighbors.

If the O'Learys did read the newspapers that day, it was probably after they did all their chores, which on this Sunday included storing a delivery of three tons of hay into their barn loft. Exhausted by the day's chores, the O'Learys went to bed at eight o'clock Sunday night. But a neighbor's party and a friend's visit made it hard for the O'Learys to get any sleep. The McLaughlins, who rented rooms from the O'Learys, were celebrating the arrival of the latest relative to make the trip from Ireland to Chicago.

A neighbor, Daniel "Peg Leg" Sullivan, stopped by to visit the O'Learys, but finding them already in bed, he crossed the street and sat on a bench to relax for awhile.

This man, whose wooden leg was made of the same combustible material that doomed the city of Chicago, was the first person to detect a fire in the O'Leary barn.

The "fireproof" Palmer House was gaining fame as one of the city's most luxurious hotels.
CHICAGO HISTORY MUSEUM, ICHI-29592, PHOTO BY P. B. GREENE

Guilty Until Proven Innocent

LIKE THE RAPIDLY spreading flames that consumed the city of Chicago, the rumors about Mrs. O'Leary's cow spread faster than the facts. Based on the sworn testimony of Daniel "Peg Leg" Sullivan, the O'Learys, and James Dalton, as well as an investigation by the Board of Police and Fire Commissioners, it's clear that the legend of Catherine O'Leary's cow was little more than a fantasy. The board's final report concluded that "there is no proof that anybody had been in the barn after nightfall that evening. Whether it originated from a spark blown from a chimney on that windy night, or was set on fire by human agency, we are unable to determine." In 1997, 127 years after the fire, the Chicago City Council passed a measure exonerating Catherine O'Leary of all responsibility.

This photograph of the O'Leary home at 137 DeKoven Street was taken shortly after the fire. Their home miraculously survived the fire that wiped out the rest of the city.

Screaming, "Fire! Fire!" Sullivan hobbled into the barn as quickly as he could. He escaped from the flames along with the frightened calf, but the barn and several other animals were not so lucky.

At about this same time, two other neighbors also became aware of the fire. James Dalton woke up the slumbering O'Learys, while William Lee sprinted to Goll's Drug Store to pull the signal at the recently installed alarm box. The alarm was supposed to send a signal to the central fire station at the courthouse building. Lee later claimed that store owner Bruno Goll refused to unlock the alarm box, saying he had already observed a fire truck racing to the scene. Goll later said he simply waited for Lee to leave before striking the alarm. Either Goll lied about sending the alarm, or the box wasn't working properly, because the signal was never received at the courthouse.

As a backup, the fire department also had a round-the-clock lookout stationed on the tower of the courthouse building. The lookout on duty that evening was Mathias Schaffer, who was giving a group of visitors a tour of his bird's-eye view of the city from atop the courthouse tower. One of the visitors noticed the smoke coming from the southwest side of the city, but Schaffer wrongly assumed it was coming from the smoldering remains of the wood mill that burned down the day before.

It wasn't until about 9:30—an hour after the blaze began—that Schaffer realized that this was a new fire. But from that distance it was hard to figure out which station was the closest. Schaffer sent firefighters from the wrong station to the wrong location. Schaffer later figured out his mistake and asked the dispatcher to send the signal to the correct station, but the dispatcher was worried that doing so would cause too much confusion and decided not to send the signal. It probably wouldn't have mattered anyway. An hour later, the fire was officially beyond control.

The fire quickly spread from house to house and business to business, consuming lumber yards and planing mills, furniture factories, box factories, paint manufacturers, warehouses, and distilleries. By this time the fire was so big that all fire stations were on call and no one was having difficulty finding it.

Most of the citizens in the southwest section of the city had begun to evacuate the area, heading across the river to the east or into the prairie on the west. Although most Chicagoans in the northern and eastern sections of the city were aware of

The courthouse as it appeared before the fire. Note the figure of a person standing on the tower platform. Perhaps it was a fire department lookout, maybe even Mathias Schaffer.

Recipe for Disaster

FIRE REQUIRES THREE ingredients: fuel, oxygen, and a spark. Although the source of the spark will never be known, the city's wooden buildings, plank sidewalks, and wooden streets provided ample fuel. And the hot southwest winds provided the oxygen that fanned the flames. Because heat rises, the fire created violent updrafts that swept sparks 100 feet into the air. The wind blew the sparks north and east, which is why the fire easily crossed streets and even the Chicago River. In an effort to deprive the fire of fuel, a group of citizens took it upon themselves to blow up homes and businesses in the fire's path. It's not clear how helpful this was.

Of all the surviving accounts of the Great Chicago Fire, only one was written by a child. In this letter to his "chum," Jason Butterfield described his family's escape from the flames. He even included a drawing of him leading his pet goat to safety.

CHICAGO HISTORY MUSEUM, ICHI-34604

the fire, few took the threat seriously. They believed that it would be stopped by the river or by gaps in buildings provided by parks or especially wide streets.

"FIRE, SIR"

One person who was slow to take the fire seriously was Mrs. Alfred Hebard, a cousin of early Chicago settler Gurdon S. Hubbard. Arriving in Chicago earlier on Sunday, Mrs. Hebard and her husband checked into the Palmer House Hotel. Learning of the fire, she later wrote, "We immediately took the elevator to the upper story of the Palmer, saw the fire, but deciding that it would not cross the river, descended to our rooms in the second story to prepare for sleep."

But Mrs. Hebard was unable to fall asleep and kept peeking through the blinds to check the progress of the fire. At one point she begged her husband "to go out and investigate once more, which he did, telling me, on his return, not to be alarmed, as there was no danger in our locality."

Mrs. Hebard reluctantly returned to bed at 11:00 P.M., but the entire family was roused about a half hour later by a knock at the door, "to which my husband responded coolly, 'What's wanted?'

Picture This

THERE ARE MANY PHOTOGRAPHS of what Chicago looked like just before and just after the fire, but amazingly there isn't a single known photograph of the fire in progress. That's probably because the large and clumsy photographic equipment of the day took too long to set up. Instead, all we have to help us imagine what the fire was like are firsthand accounts by the people who experienced and witnessed the fire, as well as illustrations of various scenes.

This sketch by Alfred R. Waud captures the fear and panic experienced while the fire raged in Chicago that night.
CHICAGO HISTORY MUSEUM, ICHI-02991

57

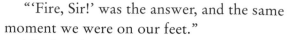

Make a Pinhole Camera

With the primitive photographic technologies available in 1871, it would have been difficult to take any pictures of a dangerous and fast-moving event like the Chicago Fire. That's because the photographer would have had to open the shutter of the camera for an extended period of time to get the proper exposure. Any objects or people moving within the frame of the shot would turn out blurry. You can make a pinhole camera to see for yourself how basic photographic technology works.

YOU'LL NEED

Cylindrical canister (tennis ball or potato chip canisters work well, especially ones with metal bottoms and clear plastic lids)

Thumbtack

Marker

Scissors or hobby knife

Clear plastic kitchen wrap (optional)

Masking tape

Black construction paper

Dark blanket

Empty and clean the canister. Using the thumbtack poke a hole into the center of the bottom of the canister. Draw a line around the outside of the cylinder, about one-fourth of the way from the bottom. Cut along the line. If your canister has a clear lid, place it onto the top of the shorter piece of the divided canister. If the lid is not clear it will be hard to see any images. Instead, place a layer of clear plastic kitchen wrap tightly over the end of the smaller half of the canister and tape to the sides.

Align the two halves of the canister so that the clear lid or kitchen wrap will be on the inside of the camera. Tape the two halves together. Wrap the canister in black construction paper and tape securely.

Go outside and experiment with looking through the camera. To block unwanted light, place the blanket over your head and camera, leaving the end with the pinhole uncovered. On a sunny day you'll be able to see images on the sides of the canister.

Notice that the images you see are upside down, because of the way light passes through the pinhole.

For instructions on how to construct a pinhole camera that can be used to take actual pictures, see *Seeing for Yourself: Techniques and Projects for Beginning Photographers* by Roger Gleason (Chicago Review Press, 1992).

"'Fire, Sir!' was the answer, and the same moment we were on our feet."

The hotel's guests were surprisingly calm about their evacuation. Their only gripe was the lack of porters to carry their trunks downstairs. But it didn't keep them from paying their bill and checking out before departing.

Once outside they may have wished that they had hurried a little more. After hiring two boys to carry their trunk, the family "sallied forth, a little before 1:00 A.M., to reach, if possible, the house of my relative, Mr. G. S. Hubbard, on LaSalle Street, a long mile and a half from the hotel. Our boys ran at full speed, and we followed, crossing State Street bridge amid a shower of coals driven by the furious wind from burning buildings and lumberyards, and seeming to be caught by an eddy were whirled in our faces."

If they thought they had reached a point of safety, they were wrong. The fire continued through the night and into the early morning of the following day, following them on their journey north. As the flames approached Gurdon Hubbard's house, a group of men "tore up carpets to cover the roof, draining both cisterns to keep the carpets wet, hoping if possible to stop the fire at that corner." But it was no use. "A wooden block nearby flashed into flame, and at 11:00 A.M. the cornice was blazing, and we were obliged to go out through the alley to escape the heat and cinders. . . ."

Another witness, Alexander Frear, a New York state legislator and Commissioner of Public Charities, was in Chicago on business. On the evening of the fire he was in the Sherman House Hotel, waiting to greet some friends of his sister's. From the lobby of the hotel he heard the court-house bells sounding the fire alarm. Nobody else in the lobby seemed overly concerned about it, so Frear did not give it much thought.

He would soon change his mind. After hearing that the fire was unusually large, Frear decided to take a look for himself. Walking south, toward his sister's home, he soon found himself walking against a human current of panicking citizens fleeing the fire. By about ten o'clock he reached the south end of the Loop, where "the cinders were falling like snowflakes in every direction and lit the street, and there was a great hubbub of men and vehicles."

Growing more anxious about the safety of his sister and her three children, Frear "started to run toward Van Buren Street, but the walks were so crowded with people

The corner of State and Madison had been the up-and-coming commercial district of the city. As the earliest stages of the clean-up process took place, horse-drawn railcars were already in service.
CHICAGO HISTORY MUSEUM, ICHI-02811

and the cinders were blown so thickly and fast that [he] found it was impossible" to see, much less to continue walking toward the fire. If he was going to reach his sister, he'd have to find another way. Frear joined a throng of Chicagoans crossing the Adams Street Bridge toward the west.

Frear later managed to work his way back to his sister's home, where he learned that his relatives had been safely removed to another location. His clothing scorched by embers, Frear collapsed in exhaustion and relief. Frear and all his relatives would survive the Great Chicago Fire.

CHICAGO IN ASHES

Many people lost all their possessions in the Chicago Fire. Wealthy business people lost fortunes, and insurance companies went out of business. Others were fortunate enough to salvage some of their prized possessions. Of course, many tried to save their homes, but as soon as that battle was lost they turned to saving smaller items. One man even went so far as to bury the family's piano in the backyard. It didn't survive. As the flames approached, some Chicagoans rushed into the streets in an attempt to hire drivers to haul their valuables to safety.

It wasn't long before newsboys hit the streets with news of the Great Fire.

The once magnificent Palmer House lies in rubble.

CHICAGO HISTORY MUSEUM, ICHI-26749.
PHOTO BY P. B. GREENE.

Plan a Fire Escape Route

There were many stories about how people tried to save their possessions during the Chicago Fire. Nowadays, people understand that the most important thing is to get to a safe place as quickly and calmly as possible. Draw a floorplan of your house and plot out escape routes in the event of a fire.

YOU'LL NEED

Paper

Pencil

Green and yellow markers

Blanket

This is something that the whole family should do together. Set up a family meeting, maybe at the dinner table. Work together on drawing a floor plan of your house. Use a separate piece of paper for each floor of the home. Make sure your floor plan shows the position of each bedroom, hallway, and stairway. Also make sure the drawing shows two exits from each room, a door and a window.

Use the green marker to draw an arrow line from your bed to the primary exit. This is the escape route you will take as long as it is not blocked by fire. Using the yellow marker, draw an arrow line from your bed to your secondary exit. If your bedroom window is on an upper floor, make sure the window leads to a safe place to wait for help—a balcony or rooftop. Repeat this process for each room, showing primary and secondary escape routes.

Share the plan with your parents and ask them to make their own suggestions. Agree on a meeting place outdoors, and assign one person who will then go to a neighbor's house to call the fire department. Ask your parents to make sure there is at least one smoke detector per floor of your home, and check them frequently to make sure the batteries are working. Replace batteries yearly.

Now for the fun part. Conduct a mock fire drill. Each kid should lie down in bed and wait for an adult to press the testing button on the smoke detector. When you hear the alarm, roll out of bed and crawl to your primary exit. (Parents can hold a blanket two feet off the ground to simulate a layer of smoke.) If you come to a closed door, feel it first to see if it's hot. If it's cool, open the door and crawl out of the house. You can also practice pretending the door is hot and crawling toward your secondary exit. Make sure parents supervise you in practicing opening the window. But don't climb out in the practice drill.

For more tips, visit the National Fire Protection Association Web site at www.nfpa.org. Kids can download and print fire escape plan grids, and teachers can order multiple copies of fire prevention and safety publications written especially for kids.

61

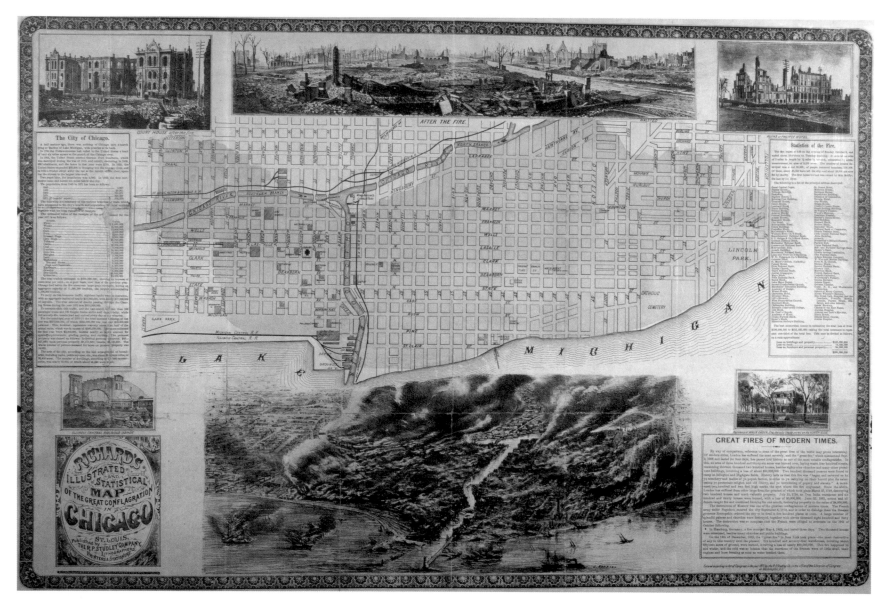

This map shows how much of the city was burned in the fire.

Alexander Frear later wrote about how people's efforts to save possessions made it harder to escape the flames:

I went through to Wabash Avenue and here the thoroughfare was utterly choked with all manner of goods and people. Everybody who had been forced from the other end of the town by the advancing flames had brought some article with him, and, as further progress was delayed, if not completely stopped by the river—the bridges of which were also choked, most of them, in their panic, abandoned their burdens, so that the streets and sidewalks presented the most astonishing wreck. Valuable oil paintings, books, pet animals, musical instruments, toys, mirrors, and bedding, were trampled under foot.

Another survivor—a young girl at the time—later recalled how she almost lost her most cherished possession. Her family was all set to leave on two fully packed wagons.

"At that moment I remembered my precious doll Bessie had been left in the playroom and instantly I jumped out and ran back to the house where I picked up Bessie in her crib and carried both away in my arms. So, we joined the long procession which was passing; mostly on foot, people carrying some special treasure in their arms (one woman had a pig) all bound Northwest."

The biggest loser in terms of personal fortune was probably William B. Ogden. A vast extent of his fortune was built on the lumber trade. He may have believed that spreading his investments between two cities, Chicago and Peshtigo, Wisconsin, was a good way to lower his risk. If disaster struck his holdings in one location, then at least the other would be intact. Unfortunately for Ogden, Peshtigo succumbed to its own great fire on the same evening that Chicago burned to the ground.

But at least Ogden came out of the fires with his life. About 300 Chicagoans and over 1,000 residents of Peshtigo were not so lucky. The lumber town situated in the middle of the Wisconsin prairie didn't know what hit it. Because it was made almost entirely of wood, Peshtigo burned even faster than Chicago, with flames traveling faster than a person could run.

The first Chicago newspaper to release an account of the Great Chicago Fire was the *Evening Journal*. The paper stated the sad facts:

An area of between six and seven miles in length and nearly a mile in width, embracing the great business part of the city, has been burned over and now lies a mass of smoldering ruins! . . . All the principal hotels, all the public buildings, all the banks, all the newspaper offices, all the places of amusement . . . nearly all the railroad depots, the water works, the gas works, several churches and thousands of private residences and stores have been consumed.

6
Reaching New Heights

E ASILY THE BIGGEST CHALLENGE ever facing Chicago was how to rebuild after the Great Chicago Fire of 1871. Obviously, nobody would ever suggest that the fire was a good thing, but it did create an opportunity that few other major cities have had: a chance to start over and build modern, wood-free structures. This opportunity attracted some of the world's most talented architects and engineers to the city and eventually resulted in the creation of a whole new architectural style, called the Chicago School of Architecture.

One of the busiest days at the world's fair was Chicago Day, celebrated on October 9, 1893, the 22nd anniversary of the Great Chicago Fire. The White City hosted 750,000 visitors on that single day.

THE NEWBERRY LIBRARY

Time Line

1872 First African American inducted to Chicago Police Department; first woman admitted to state bar, Chicago Public Library created

1874 Workingmen's Party of Illinois established

1877 Knights of Labor establish Chicago branch

1879 Art Institute of Chicago opens to the public; Chicago Bicycle Club established

1880 Chicago population passes 500,000

1881 Marshall Field & Company opens for business

1882 Chicago Stock Exchange established

1884 Central Labor Union and Illinois State Federation of Labor established

1886 Haymarket riot takes place

1889 Jane Addams opens Hull House

1890 Chicago population passes one million

1891 University of Chicago and Chicago Symphony Orchestra established

1892 First elevated "L" trains begin operating in Chicago

1893 Chicago hosts World's Columbian Exposition

1894 The Field Museum of Natural History opens

"In the midst of a calamity without parallel in the world's history, looking upon the ashes of thirty years' accumulations, the people of this once beautiful city have resolved that Chicago Shall Rise Again."

—JOSEPH MEDILL, IN THE *CHICAGO TRIBUNE*, OCTOBER 11, 1871

W. D. Kerfoot was the first to open a real estate office in the burnt district. A sign posted on the building reads, "All gone but Wife Children and Energy."

WOOD-FREE ZONE

It seems hard to believe, but the first buildings to go up after the fire were made of wood. But these were only for temporary shelter and office space until more long-term structures could be built. Wood barracks built in what is now Washington Square Park provided shelter for some of Chicago's 100,000 post-fire homeless.

Shortly after the fire, the city passed an ordinance banning the construction of wood frame buildings in much of Chicago. The boundaries were from 39th Street on the south, Western Avenue on the west, Fullerton Avenue on the north, and Lake Michigan on the east.

It wasn't easy for Chicagoans to get back on their feet after the fire. It helped to be well-insured or to have political connections. Chicago's wealthiest citizens were soon rebuilding their hotels, stores, warehouses, and factories. In keeping with the will to come back bigger, better, and stronger, many of the buildings were more magnificent than the ones they replaced.

John Drake lost several hotels in the fire but acquired another one for a bargain. As the fire approached the Michigan Avenue Hotel, Drake darted into the front door and offered to buy the seemingly doomed building. The previous owner accepted

One Giant Step Back

SOMETIMES YOU NEED to take one step back before you can take two forward. No doubt about it, the Chicago Fire was quite a setback. But the way in which Chicagoans rose to the occasion and rebuilt their city is one of the world's most incredible stories. The post-fire rebuilding of Chicago put the city's motto of "I Will" on magnificent display. Throughout the city, workers began clearing rubble and collecting reusable bricks. Children scavenged for fire relics, which they sold to souvenir hunters. Before the city even stopped smoldering, one young couple actually got married, exchanging vows in the midst of the ruins.

You might think that the population would have gone down after the devastation of the fire. It actually skyrocketed—from 300,000 in 1870 to 500,000 in 1880. By 1890 Chicago would be the second largest city in the United States, with a population of over one million. One reason the city's population surged in this period was that Chicago quadrupled in geographic size. In 1889 Chicago annexed Lake, Jefferson, Lake View, and Hyde Park townships.

The stores and hotels Potter Palmer owned along State Street were a complete loss. The newly rebuilt Palmer House, pictured here in the 1880s, became the city's largest hotel.

CHICAGO HISTORY MUSEUM, ICHI-24733, PHOTO BY KAUFMANN & FABRY

First Impression

JOURNALIST AND novelist Theodore Dreiser moved to Chicago in 1884, when rebuilding was in full swing. Here are his first impressions of the city, which he called "a veritable miracle of pleasing sensations and fascinating scenes."

The spirit of Chicago flowed into me and made me ecstatic. Its personality was different from anything I had ever known; it was compound of hope and joy in existence, intense hope and intense joy. . . . The odor and flavor of the city, the vastness of its reaches, seemed to speak or sing or tinkle like a living, breathing thing. It came to me again with inexpressible variety and richness . . .

—from *Dawn* (1931) by Theodore Dreiser

Chicago is famous for its elevated train tracks, which today carry a half million passengers throughout the city on a typical weekday. The "L" trains first rattled above ground in 1893. This pile of iron shows the L tracks before they were assembled.
COURTESY OF KENAN HEISE

68

Drake's offer and may have even chuckled to himself on his way out. But Drake got the last laugh when the building somehow survived the fire unscathed. In 1873 Drake also opened another property, the magnificent Grand Pacific Hotel.

THE CHICAGO SCHOOL OF ARCHITECTURE

The most impressive innovation to come out of Chicago's post-fire rebuilding was the skyscraper. Before the Chicago Fire, ten-story buildings were unheard of. After the fire, a rapid growth in population caused land prices to swell. To get the most usable space out of a parcel of land, architects designed buildings that soared higher into the air than ever before. The first skyscrapers to rise from the ashes of the fire were built using a traditional construction technique. The outside walls were made of stone blocks (masonry) piled one on top of the other. These blocks provided the main structural support for these early skyscrapers.

Daniel Burnham and his partner John Wellborn Root built a number of these early skyscrapers, including the first building called a skyscraper, the Montauk Building (1882), the Rookery (1888), and the northern half of the Monadnock Building (1891). But

there was a problem. In order to support the weight of the taller buildings, the walls had to be made thicker and thicker at the bottom. These thick walls were a waste of valuable indoor space, putting architects back to square one: they were still wasting the expensive land these buildings were standing on.

The first architect to get around this new problem was William Le Baron Jenney, who is credited with building the first modern skyscraper, the Home Insurance Building (1885). Instead of supporting the building's weight with thicker and thicker stone walls, Jenney constructed a metal framework which was then covered up with "curtain walls" of brick and stone. This innovation made possible Chicago's oldest skyscrapers, as well as Chicago's future giants, such as the John Hancock Center and the Sears Tower.

What really set the Chicago School of Architecture apart was that its architects combined practical innovations with style. No other architectural firm blended function and form better than Adler & Sullivan. Dankmar Adler was the engineer who focused more on the physical structure of the buildings they designed, while his partner Louis Sullivan made sure the buildings were not only useful but beautiful.

Going Up

BEFORE THE ERA of skyscrapers, buildings in Chicago rarely rose above two or three floors high. One reason was that no one wanted to climb that many flights of stairs. The development of efficient and safe elevators at about this time made Chicago's early skyscrapers possible and practical.

Adler & Sullivan's triumphs include the Auditorium Building (1889), which still stands at the northwest corner of Congress and Michigan Avenues, and the Chicago Stock Exchange (1893), which was demolished in 1972 over the protests of preservationists. Sullivan also designed the Transportation Building for the 1893 Columbian Exposition's White City.

PRAIRIE SCHOOL OF ARCHITECTURE

Not all of Chicago's innovations in architecture belong to the bigger-is-better school of thought. Unlike the designers of soaring skyscrapers, architects like Frank

Architectural Walking Tour: The First Skyscrapers

There's only so much you can learn about architecture from a book. To get a full appreciation of a building you need to stand in front it, walk around it, go inside. Get your parents or teachers to organize a trip downtown to see a few of Chicago's architectural treasures.

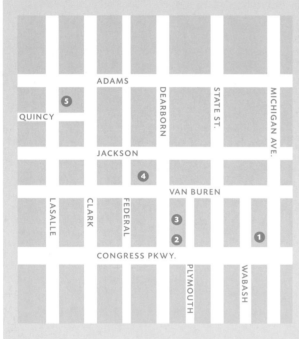

As you walk the route of the tour below, consider the following questions:

What are the building's physical characteristics? How many stories does it have? What building materials were used?

How would you describe the style? Classical or modern? Sleek or bulky? Ornate or plain? Do doorways and windows have curved arches or are they square/rectangular? Is the design symmetrical or imbalanced?

The tour should take approximately two hours. Start at the northwest corner of Congress Parkway and Michigan Avenue.

Auditorium Building (1)

430 S. Michigan Ave.
Architects: Adler & Sullivan (1889)

Tours of the Auditorium Theatre can be arranged by calling (312) 431-2389, ext. 0.

The massive stone arches on Congress are one of the most impressive features of this imposing structure. The main floor lobby (formerly of the 400-room hotel, now of Roosevelt University) can be accessed from the Michigan Avenue entrance.

Notice the mosaic tile floors and arched doorways. As you climb the grand staircase to the second floor, look up at the stained glass ceiling. Be sure to take the elevator to the seventh floor to visit Ganz Recital Hall (previously the hotel's lavish banquet hall and ballroom). Then take the elevator to the 10th floor to see the library (formerly the hotel's dining room). The east windows provide a wide open view of Grant Park and Lake Michigan.

From the west side of the building (Wabash and Congress), walk three blocks west, to the corner of Congress and Dearborn. Turn right. The Manhattan Building is on the northeast corner of Dearborn and Congress.

Manhattan Building (2)

431 S. Dearborn St.
Architect: William Le Baron Jenney (1891)

When the Manhattan Building was constructed, no other building in the United States had so many floors. Count how many stories high the building is. Also, notice how the windows stick out beyond the face of the building. These are called bay windows. Without any supports beneath them, what do you think is holding them up? It's called a cantilever. A cantilever is a structural element that is only secured on one end, like a horizontal beam that extends beyond a column or wall. What do you think is the advantage of a bay window?

Walk north two buildings.

Old Colony Building (3)
407 S. Dearborn
Architects: Holabird & Roche (1894)

The first thing most people notice about this building is that it has rounded corners, which increases the interior space and the amount of natural light that can enter the building.

Walk north, crossing Van Buren. Stop halfway between Van Buren and Jackson. Look across the street to the west.

Monadnock Building (4)
53 W. Jackson
Architects: Burnham & Root (1889–91)
54 W. Van Buren Addition
Architects: Holabird & Roche (1893)

Start by looking up. See if you can notice the dividing line between the original half of the building (north) and the addition (south). The southern half has a cornice that the north portion lacks. And the window bays are slightly different on each half. Also try to identify where the exterior walls become thicker (northern half). Cross Dearborn Street at Van Buren and look at the Monadnock's profile. Why do you think the building curves inward on the way up? Enter the building from the Van Buren entrance. Walk along the main corridor south to north. As you go, notice how the thicker walls reduce the amount of main-floor interior space in the shops to your right.

Exit the building on Jackson and turn left. Walk west three blocks to LaSalle. Turn right and walk north one block to Quincy Avenue. The Rookery is on the northeast corner of LaSalle and Quincy.

The Rookery (5)
209 S. LaSalle
Architects: Burnham & Root (1885–88)
Lobbies renovated by Frank Lloyd Wright (1907)

The Rookery is built on the same spot where the old City Hall used to be. Apparently, the City Hall building was home to families of rooks, similar to crows. It was also home to self-serving politicians who were compared to the noisy black birds. That's how the Rookery got its name. Can you find any images of birds in the building's design?

Be sure to go inside to see the glass-roofed court-yard. Many changes were made to the Rookery over the years, including renovations (updates) and restorations (removing the updates). In the most recent restorations, several of the architect's original designs were displayed. See if you can find John Wellborn Root's original wrought-iron columns hidden beneath Frank Lloyd Wright's marble panels. Also see if you can find the small square showing the original mosaic flooring.

Old Meets New

WHEN IT WAS COMPLETED, the 16-story Monadnock was the tallest building in the world. Built in two phases, the northern portion (finished in 1891) was constructed using weight-bearing masonry walls that were six feet thick. The southern portion (finished in 1893), though it looks roughly the same from the outside, was built using a steel frame covered with a "curtain" of terra-cotta (a fire-hardened clay).

The Frederick C. Robie House, pictured here in 1963, is undergoing a multimillion-dollar restoration.
LIBRARY OF CONGRESS, HABS ILL,16-CHIG,33-4

Lloyd Wright set out to design buildings that fit into their surroundings. Ideas and designs put forth by Wright and other like-minded architects came to be known as the Prairie School of architecture. Although the Prairie School placed more emphasis on horizontal lines than the vertical lines of the Chicago School's skyscrapers, the results were no less dramatic.

On the South Side of Chicago, in the Hyde Park neighborhood near the University of Chicago, sits one of Wright's most ingenious buildings, the Frederick C. Robie House (1909). Designed for the owner of a bicycle and motorcycle factory, the Robie House proves that even a three-story building can be breathtaking. The roof line hangs so far beyond the house that it's hard to figure out what's keeping it from collapsing.

Wright didn't spend his entire career in Chicago, however. One of his most noteworthy designs—and the one he's most famous for—was built in Pennsylvania. Known as Fallingwater, the house is so completely incorporated into its natural setting that a stream actually flows through it.

MAY DAY

Chicago was undergoing a miraculous rebirth, but not everyone benefited from it. For every Pullman, McCormick, Palmer, and Field, there were tens of thousands of everyday people who did hard, physical labor—and got paid very little for it. This was before federal laws protected workers from unsafe working conditions. Unable to make a decent living, some workers responded by forming unions. A union is an organization of workers whose goal is to negotiate with business owners for better pay and working conditions. When unions don't get their way, they sometimes also organize protests and rallies. A union's biggest weapon is to go on strike—to stop working until their demands are met.

In a series of marches and rallies taking place in Chicago, workers demanded an

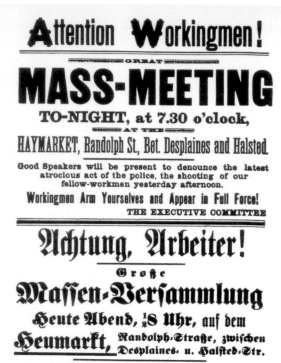

This poster encouraged Chicago workers to gather at Haymarket Square to protest labor conditions.
COURTESY OF KENAN HEISE

eight-hour workday. On May 1, 1886, more than 30,000 workers went on strike. Over the next few days, striking workers and police clashed on the streets. On May 4, 1886, workers gathered in Chicago's Haymarket Square to protest police violence. When police moved in to break up the peaceful demonstration, someone lobbed a bomb into the crowd. Eight policemen and a number of protesters died, some from the fighting that followed the explosion.

Eight defendants were found guilty of murder, even though there was no evidence of their guilt. Four of these defendants were hanged and a fifth committed suicide. The three remaining defendants were pardoned by Illinois Governor John Altgeld in 1893. To this day, workers worldwide celebrate May Day on May 1 to commemorate the struggle for fair working conditions.

THE WHITE CITY

No single event marked Chicago's triumphant comeback from the fire as dramatically as the World's Columbian Exposition. Held in 1893—just 22 years after the fire—the fair commemorated the 400th anniversary of Columbus's discovery of the Americas (one year late). The World's Columbian Exposition would be the biggest and most ambitious world's fair to date. The newly rebuilt city of Chicago was a great attraction all by itself, but the planners also built an entirely new temporary city to greet the 27 million visitors who came to the fair. The fairgrounds were commonly called the White City, because the buildings were all constructed of bright white plaster.

As chief architect and planner of the White City, Daniel H. Burnham supervised the construction of a temporary stand-alone city with more than 200 buildings. The Manufactures and Liberal Arts Building was the largest covered structure in the world when it was built with over one million square feet of indoor space.

In addition to all the buildings, the White City needed all the other things a city needs: its own water purification and sewage system, as well as its own power plant. It would need a fire department and police force. It needed walkways designed to prevent human traffic jams, as well as shady rest areas to provide relief from the hot summer sun. It needed enough restaurants to feed as many as 750,000 daily visitors.

Several new food items made their debut at the fair. With limited dining space, as well as a limited amount of time to see all the wonders of the fair, fairgoers preferred foods that could be eaten on the go. A caramel-

August Spies (top left), pictured here with four other "anarchists," was accused of being the leader of the Haymarket Riot.

An illustration of the White City, its buildings, waterways, and attractions.

covered popcorn and peanut snack, later named Cracker Jack, was introduced at the fair. So was the idea of placing a sausage on a bun—what is now called the hot dog. Quaker Oats, shredded wheat, Aunt Jemima pancake mix, and Wrigley's Juicy Fruit gum were also introduced at the fair. And the blue ribbon for best beer at the fair was awarded to Pabst. The company was so proud of its achievement that the award has since been part of the product's name: Pabst Blue Ribbon Beer.

In addition to feeding the fairgoers and making them comfortable, organizers spent a great deal of time coming up with ways to entertain fairgoers. The nearby Midway Plaisance (a mile-long grass avenue) was the site for attractions like snake charmers, belly dancers, and the world's first Ferris wheel.

When the architects were planning the grounds of the Columbian Exposition, they wanted to come up with something original. In fact they wanted to "out-Eiffel" the Eiffel Tower, which had been built for the Paris World's Fair four years earlier in 1889. After reviewing many plans, Burnham

Buffalo Bill Cody's Wild West Show was performed near the fair. The show included reenactments of battles between cowboys and Indians, as well as of a bison hunt and a train robbery.

Chicagoans gathered on Dearborn Street for a parade celebrating the opening of the World's Columbian Exposition.

agreed to give a young bridge builder from Pittsburgh a chance to make his name. George W. Ferris designed and constructed what turned out to be the most popular attraction at the fair.

Here's how journalist Marian Shaw described the experience of riding the first Ferris wheel: "Now we find ourselves in the shadow of the wonderful Ferris wheel, from the top of which, 260 feet above terra-firma, we may view . . . the whole of Jackson Park, Chicago with its suburbs, miles and miles of the blue expanse of Lake Michigan, the states of Wisconsin, Michigan, and Indiana, and far into the interior of Illinois."

THE WORLD'S CULTURES ON DISPLAY

The Midway Plaisance was also where fair organizers placed a number of exhibits displaying the different cultures of the world. The project started out as a serious and well-intentioned scientific project. Anthropologist Frederick Ward Putnam wanted to study and preserve various "primitive" cultures of the American continents before they vanished. Putnam sent teams of researchers out across the Americas "from Alaska to Tierra del Fuego" (from the northern-most regions of North America to the southernmost regions

The first Ferris wheel was a main attraction at the World's Columbian Exposition in 1893.
THE NEWBERRY LIBRARY

Original Ferris Wheel Dimensions

Capacity:	2,160 riders
Passenger cars:	36
Height:	264 feet
Wheel diameter:	250 feet
Circumference:	825 feet
Axle:	45 feet
Support towers:	140 feet

of South America). His teams were instructed to collect artifacts, record languages, and observe behaviors. Some of the field workers even managed to persuade entire tribes to make the trip to Chicago for the fair.

Unfortunately, because of racial stereotypes and a desire to attract more paying visitors, these exhibits were not very authentic, and in some cases downright offensive. For example, at the "Eskimaux Village" members of an Inuit tribe were coerced into wearing traditional clothing, even though the summer temperatures in Chicago made them very uncomfortable.

But the artifacts collected on these expeditions were eventually put to good

Make Homemade Caramel Corn

The challenge of feeding so many people at the world's fair was met in part by the introduction of quickly prepared foods that could be enjoyed while strolling through the fairgrounds. In addition to the hamburger and hot dog, a new popcorn and peanut snack was a big hit.

The snack that was introduced at the World's Columbian Exposition eventually came to be known as Cracker Jack. It became a part of popular culture when it was included in the lyrics of the song "Take Me Out to the Ballgame" in 1908. The introduction of the "Prize in Every Box" came four years later.

Try making this simple version of the snack at home.

Adult supervision required. Use oven mitts when removing items from the microwave oven.

INGREDIENTS

1 bag microwave popcorn

¼ cup peanuts

4 tablespoons butter or margarine

4 tablespoons brown sugar

1 tablespoon honey

1. Pop the popcorn following the instructions on the bag. Mix with peanuts in a large bowl and set aside.

2. Place the butter in a medium-sized microwavable bowl, and microwave until melted (about 45 seconds).

3. Add the brown sugar and honey. Stir until the brown sugar is dissolved.

4. Microwave the sauce until bubbly (about one minute).

5. Stir the sauce into the popcorn and peanuts mixture, coating all contents evenly.

6. Let the caramel corn cool for at least five minutes before eating.

Build a Model of the Original Ferris Wheel

With all the high-speed, head-whipping roller coasters out there these days, the Ferris wheel probably seems pretty tame to most modern-day thrill seekers. But when it was introduced at the 1893 World's Columbian Exposition, there was nothing like it. In fact, some people were so terrified by the idea of riding it that they fainted. No wonder: at 264 feet high, the Ferris wheel would have taken most riders higher off the ground than they had ever been. Once onlookers overcame their fears, the Ferris wheel became one of the fair's most popular attractions. Approximately one and a half million fairgoers took a spin on the first Ferris wheel.

Adult supervision required

YOU'LL NEED

10 sheets of 8½ x 11-inch heavy (110 lb.) card-stock paper; paper needs to be rigid enough to stand up straight, but pliable enough to be rolled into tubes without creasing

Pencil

Ruler

Hobby knife or scissors

Transparent tape

The Outer Wheels

Using the heavy cardstock paper, make two photocopies of the circular template on the following page. Cut out the wheels, making sure to leave the tabs intact. It's usually easier to use scissors for the outer cuts and a hobby knife for the inner cuts. If you are using a hobby knife, make sure the work surface below the paper you're cutting will not be damaged by the blade going through the paper. Set the wheels aside.

The Main Supports

Photocopy the support template at right onto a piece of heavy card stock. Cut out. Fold another piece of the card stock in half to make a rectangle of 8½ x 5½ inches. Align the top edge of the support template with the folded hinge. Trace the outer edges of the template onto the folded paper. Cut out the support, fold at dotted line. Repeat this process one more time, to make two supports.

Ferris Wheel Axle

Cut a square from the card stock with four equal sides of 3 inches. Place a pencil along one of the edges and roll the paper into a small tube. Tape securely, and slide the pencil out. Using your thumb and index finger, crimp the ends of the tube.

Assembly

Insert one end of the axle through the center hole of each of the outer wheels, so that a little bit of the axle extends beyond each wheel. Bend the outer wheel tabs in and tape together.

Set the wheel assembly into the support cradle.

SUPPORT TEMPLATE

Bertha Honoré Palmer (1849–1918) headed up the World's Columbian Exposition's Board of Lady Managers. Mrs. Palmer was also an avid art collector. Her collection of European paintings was later donated to the Art Institute of Chicago.

ANDERS LEONARD ZORN, SWEDISH, 1860–1920, *MRS. POTTER PALMER*, 1893, OIL ON CANVAS, 258 X 141.2 CM, POTTER PALMER COLLECTION, 1922.450, THE ART INSTITUTE OF CHICAGO, PHOTOGRAPHY © THE ART INSTITUTE OF CHICAGO.

use after the fair. The Field Museum was established in 1894 to showcase the many artifacts collected from around the world for the World's Columbian Exposition. Its first home was in the former Palace of Fine Arts Building, one of the only permanent buildings constructed for the fair. In 1921 the Field Museum moved from Chicago's South Side to its current home in Grant Park.

Today, the Field Museum continues to build its reputation as a world-class natural history museum and research center. Most Chicagoans fondly recall annual field trips to the Field Museum, where they could see the giant long-tusked elephants, towering totem poles, and later the famous *T. rex* named Sue. But the Field is also an active scientific institution that organizes archaeological digs and anthropological field work all over the world.

A CHANCE TO SHINE

The World's Columbian Exposition was important for many reasons, including the opportunity it gave women to show that they were just as capable as men. Back before women could vote and before very many of them enjoyed professional careers, women played a major role in planning aspects of the fair. Led by Bertha Palmer,

wife of hotel owner Potter Palmer, the Board of Lady Managers showed what an intelligent and determined group of women could do if given a chance. They sponsored a competition to hire a female architect to design the Woman's Building. The winner was Sophia Hayden, a young graduate of MIT, who designed a "graceful and classic" Italian renaissance villa.

Opportunities were created for women journalists, too, who visited the fair in large numbers to describe the wonders of Chicago and the exposition to readers all across the country. One such writer, Marian Shaw, called the Woman's Building a "monument of the best the world has to show of human progress, since it [signifies] the emancipation of woman. . . ." With exhibits demonstrating "woman's achievements in every branch of industry," Shaw said the Woman's Building presented "an unanswerable argument to those who have been wont to deny her ability to excel in any line of work outside that of light fancy work or household drudgery."

But the fair did not provide opportunities for all Americans. African Americans were excluded from the planning and festivities of the fair. All of their proposals for exhibits were rejected by white board members. Frederick Douglass and Ida B. Wells organized protests and delivered speeches

Ida B. Wells (1862–1931).
COURTESY OF KENAN HEISE

about the unfair treatment. They also wrote a pamphlet called *The Reason Why the Colored American Is Not in the World's Columbian Exposition*.

FOUL PLAY AT THE FAIR

Between the amusements offered and the amazing technological exhibits on display, Chicago's World's Fair created great amounts of excitement and optimism for the future

of humankind. But the fair also attracted people with bad intentions. Crime was high, with pickpockets and con artists preying on tourists. Some people who came to the fair disappeared and were never heard from again, most likely the victims of murder.

The most disturbing crimes committed during the fair were performed by Herman Webster Mudgett, who could be called the first serial killer in the United States. Using the name H. H. Holmes, Mudgett masqueraded as a doctor and pharmacist. He opened a pharmacy on the South Side of Chicago and also a hotel catering to tourists visiting the fair. A number of people, especially young women who stayed there, eventually disappeared. By the time Mudgett confessed to his crimes in 1896, he had killed 27 people.

Another sensational murder occurred a few days before the fair ended. A deranged man assassinated Chicago Mayor Carter Harrison on October 28. The murder of this popular mayor shocked the city. It also cast a dark shadow on the closing ceremonies, which were supposed to be a grand celebration of the city's accomplishments.

In spite of its drawbacks, the fair was considered by many an amazing success. It attracted millions of visitors to Chicago from the rest of the country and world, and it even turned a small profit.

Chicago Gets Cultured

IN ADDITION TO the Field Museum of Natural History, a number of cultural institutions were created around the turn of the 19th century, including the Chicago Public Library (1873), which was made possible by the many books donated from all parts of the world to the city after the Great Chicago Fire. The Art Institute of Chicago was established in 1879, and the current building it occupies was built in 1893. The Newberry Library opened its doors in 1887. Both the Ravinia Music Festival and Orchestra Hall opened in 1904.

AFTER THE FAIR

Having successfully met the challenges of building the White City, Burnham proved himself the perfect candidate to help Chicago plan its future growth. Thirteen years after the fair, in 1906, the city was showing signs that it may have grown too quickly. Chicago was crowded, dingy, noisy, and polluted. Teaming up with Edward Bennett, Burnham unveiled his Plan of Chicago in 1909. It is the best example of

> "Make no little plans, they have no magic to stir men's blood. . . . Make big plans . . . remembering that a noble logical diagram once recorded will never die." —DANIEL BURNHAM

The Chicago White Stockings, circa 1877, before they came to be known as the Cubs.

what he considered "big plans." Burnham's plan called for wider streets, some running diagonally from the city's downtown to the outlying areas northwest and southwest. It also recommended improving Chicago's existing parks and creating new ones.

Not all of Burnham's plans were followed, but many of the unique features of modern Chicago came from the Plan of Chicago, including Grant Park, Northerly Island, a double-decked Wacker Drive, and Navy Pier. The city eventually followed through on Burnham's suggestion to straighten a crooked segment of the Chicago River.

BEFORE "WAIT 'TIL NEXT YEAR"

These days the Cubs are known as the "lovable losers" who at the end of each unsuccessful season can only say, "wait 'til next year." It wasn't always that way. In fact, they weren't even always known as the Cubs. Back in their earlier years—when they were called the Chicago White Stockings— the team dominated the professional base-

ball scene. They won numerous pennants and world championships in the late 1800s and early 1900s. The White Stockings took their first pennant in 1876 behind the leadership of pitcher Albert Goodwill Spalding and the versatile player-manager Adrian "Cap" Anson. Outfielder Ross Barnes batted .429 that year, a team record that will never be broken.

Baseball was a different game back then. Believe it or not, in the first years of base-ball, fielders didn't even wear baseball mitts. Switching from pitcher to playing first base, Spalding was the first baseball star to use a leather glove in the field. When others quickly followed, Spalding made a good living selling his own brand of glove at his Chicago sporting goods store. This was the birth of the Spalding sporting goods brand name that's still in business today.

In the early years of baseball, White Stockings players and coaches pioneered a number of other innovations that influenced the game for years to come, including the curve ball, catcher's signals to the pitcher,

and the practice of rotating pitchers. Changing pitchers proved especially effective back when most teams would have only one or two pitchers, and the best one was expected to pitch every inning of every game, unless he was sick, injured, or giving up too many runs. It's no surprise that pitchers would last only a couple of seasons

This depiction of a baseball game in the 1880s shows fielders without leather mitts.

LIBRARY OF CONGRESS, LC-USZC4-2776

ADRIAN C. ANSON.
ALLEN & GINTER'S
Cigarettes.
RICHMOND. VIRGINIA

Adrian Cap Anson (1852–1922), shown here in 1887, was an early star on the mighty Chicago White Stockings.
LIBRARY OF CONGRESS

before their arms wore out. Cap Anson's more rested pitching staff was one reason the White Stockings won the pennant three straight years from 1880 to 1882.

In 1882 the White Stockings played in their first postseason championship series, tying the American Association's Cincinnati Reds 1–1. This was before the league figured out that it was better to play an odd number of games to eliminate a tie.

In 1884 the league made a rule change that would have a huge impact on the game for years to come. From then on, when a batter hit a ball over the outfield fence it would be ruled a home run, instead of a ground-rule double. The White Stockings hit the most home runs in the National League that year but still finished in fifth place.

The White Stockings returned to form, taking the pennant in 1885 and 1886, but they failed to win either of the postseason championships against the St. Louis Browns. They didn't call it the World Series back then, and the players didn't take it very seriously either. It wasn't unusual for the two teams to secretly split the prize money evenly, so there was little motivation to win. The White Stockings would not win another pennant for 20 years.

7

The Haves and the Have-Nots

T HE WONDERS OF CHICAGO at the turn of the century, complete with the miraculous postfire rebuilding and the World's Fair, might make some think that it would have been cool to experience it all firsthand. Maybe yes, and maybe no. It would all depend on whether or not you were wealthy enough to enjoy the city's wonders and to avoid the city's dangers.

Sure, life was good for the likes of wealthy Chicagoans, such as the families of hotel owner Potter Palmer, retail giant Marshall Field, sleeper railcar manufacturer George Pullman, and slaughterhouse owners Philip Armour and Augustus Swift. Things were

This photograph, taken in the late 1880s, shows waiters preparing to serve a meal at the Palmer House Grand Dining Room.
CHICAGO HISTORY MUSEUM, ICHI-00748. PHOTO BY J. W. TAYLOR.

Time Line

1902 Potter Palmer dies

1905 *Chicago Defender* newspaper founded; Industrial Workers of the World, a radical labor union, established in Chicago

1906 Marshall Field dies

1907 State of Illinois establishes the Department of Factory Inspection

1910 The Chicago branch of the National Association for the Advancement of Colored People (NAACP) is established

1911 Illinois legislature passes the Occupational Disease Act and the Workmen's Compensation Act, legislation designed to protect workers' health, safety, and rights

1913 Illinois legislature permits Illinois women to vote in local and national elections, seven years earlier than women got the vote nationwide

1914 Weeghman Field constructed (later renamed Wrigley Field); Tinkertoys introduced in Evanston, Illinois

1915 Chicago elects its first African American alderman, Oscar DePriest

1916 Carl Sandburg's *Chicago Poems* published; Chicago Cubs move to new home field at Clark and Addison

1917 White Sox win the World Series

also good for middle-class business people, those who could afford decent housing, nutritious meals, and even some of the city's entertainments, like plays, musical theater, concerts, and dance halls.

On the other hand, life was hardly a walk in the park for most Chicagoans living in the late 1800s and early 1900s. Poverty, disease, and malnutrition were the harsh realities of lives lived in the shadows of the White City. The rich lived in twenty-room mansions on Prairie Avenue, while many of the people who labored in their factories were crammed into the city's slums.

Many of Chicago's poor were recent immigrants from foreign countries. As of 1850 more than half of Chicago's residents were foreign born. This first wave of immigrants came mostly from northwestern European countries like England, Ireland, Scotland, Germany, Sweden, Norway, and Holland. These immigrants tended to be Protestants.

By 1900 foreign-born immigrants made up 77 percent of Chicago's population. The second wave of immigrants came largely from southeastern Europe: Italians, Poles, Lithuanians, Slavic peoples, Hungarians, and Russians. These immigrants were more likely to be Catholic or Jewish and were less likely to speak English. These newer

Living the Good Life

FOR KIDS LIKE GEORGE AND FANNY GLESSNER, the 1880s and 1890s were a wonderful time to be a kid living in Chicago. Their family was rich, and they had all the comforts and advantages money could buy. John Jacob Glessner made a fortune when his farm equipment company was bought by the McCormick Reaper Company. The Glessners moved to Chicago and built their Prairie Avenue mansion in 1887. The children were taught at home by private tutors, and George would go on to attend Harvard University.

George and Fanny Glessner.
GLESSNER HOUSE MUSEUM

The Glessner House, just after construction was completed in 1887.
GLESSNER HOUSE MUSEUM

immigrants were often resented and discriminated against by the native-born Americans, as well as the earlier immigrants. As a result the later immigrants usually took whatever menial jobs they could find. Because these jobs paid low wages, several families often shared living spaces that were made for one family.

Sometimes as many as 40 people from different families shared the same three-room unit in an overcrowded apartment building. Many of these ramshackle homes, called tenement buildings, had no running water, no toilets, and no baths. Some didn't even have windows. The alleys behind them were overrun with garbage, sewage, and rats. Tenement housing was a breeding ground for disease.

Many of Chicago's poor immigrants were unemployed or had very low-paying jobs. They usually worked long hours, 10 hours a day, 6 days a week. For this they were paid about 10 dollars. That works out to less than 45 dollars a month, and the average rent for people living in Chicago's slums was 8 to 10 dollars a month. There was little money left for food, clothing, and other necessities. Certainly, people living on these kinds of wages didn't earn enough to spend on luxuries or to save for the future.

"I have struck a city—a real city—and they call it Chicago. . . . Having seen it, I urgently desire never to see it again. It is inhabited by savages. Its water is [filthy], and its air is dirt."

—RUDYARD KIPLING, 1899

Kids living in Chicago's slums play leap-frog in a garbage-filled alley.

Create a Photographic Documentary of Your Home/Neighborhood

When George Glessner was growing up in Chicago one of his hobbies was photography. Thanks to George, the Glessner House is one of the few house museums in the United States with a photographic record of what the house and neighborhood looked like back when it was occupied by its original owners.

Pretend you are creating a photographic documentary of your home and neighborhood for future generations of historians and readers to look at. Using your family camera (or a disposable camera), take photographs of your house and neighborhood. Make sure to take a picture of your bedroom and dining room. Outside, take a picture of the front of your house from across the front sidewalk, your front yard, backyard, street, and any other interesting landmarks in your neighborhood. Assemble the pictures in a scrapbook and share them with classmates or neighborhood friends.

George Glessner's bedroom. Notice the sign—"Hands Off"—and the telegraph system his father installed so that George could send "instant" messages to his wealthy pals.

GLESSNER HOUSE MUSEUM

Looking south from the corner of Prairie Avenue and 18th Street.

GLESSNER HOUSE MUSEUM

The view across Prairie Avenue toward Lake Michigan from George Glessner's bedroom window.
GLESSNER HOUSE MUSEUM

The Glessners' dining room.
GLESSNER HOUSE MUSEUM

On the back porch of the Glessner House, George Glessner took this picture of his mother's friends who were at the house for a literary discussion.
GLESSNER HOUSE MUSEUM

Instead of going to school, this young boy helped his family survive by selling matches and flypaper on the streets of Chicago.

Second Thoughts

THE WRITER THEODORE DREISER, who was so dazzled by the wonders of Chicago in the 1880s, later developed a more somber view of life in the big city. As a reporter for the *Chicago Globe* in 1891, Dreiser got his first "real contact with life—murders, arson . . . bribery, corruption, trickery, and false witness in every conceivable form." Below Dreiser described his reactions to a newspaper article he read about a "tall, thin, and emaciated" man who "dropped dead" on a city street.

One of the most commonplace items of this, our city life, is one like the above, which records the falling from exhaustion, or the death by starvation, of someone who has reached the limit of his physical ability to cope with life. It is no longer a notable thing. The papers give it no more than a passing mention. . . . [T]his brief way of recording the failure of an individual . . . is so characteristic of the city, and of life as a whole. Nature is so grim. The city, which represents it so effectively, is also grim. It does not care at all.

—from "The Man on the Sidewalk" (1909) by Theodore Dreiser

Large families relied on able-bodied adults to work, but because many of the jobs available to poor immigrants were dangerous, an injury or illness could easily ruin a family. Children of poor families that couldn't make ends meet might wind up in an orphanage—if they survived at all. With disease and not enough food, a child born into Chicago's slums would be lucky to reach the age of four.

Many children had to work to help their parents make money. In Illinois it was illegal to employ children under the age of 14 in a factory. Some employers ignored the law, and desperate families lied about their children's ages. Also, the law did not prevent children from doing nonfactory jobs. Young girls often did sewing work at home, and young boys sold merchandise on the street.

FROM HERO TO VILLAIN

George Pullman had once been considered a hero in Chicago, for the ingenious way he raised many of Chicago's buildings to the new higher street level. Later, he won the praises of many for the luxurious Pullman Palace Cars his company built. As his company grew Pullman decided to build his own company town several miles south of Chicago. The town of Pullman was designed to provide affordable, reliable labor for the construction of his railroad freight cars and luxury sleeper cars. Pullman was a company town, and George Pullman owned everything in it, including the factory and workshops, the schools, hotels, grocery stores, and even the apartments rented to workers. Pullman paid slightly higher wages to his workers, but he also charged higher rental rates, which he deducted from his workers' paychecks.

As long as business was good, there were few complaints. But in 1894 the economy fell into a depression. In a weak economy orders for luxury sleeper cars went down. Pullman reduced his workers' hours and pay rates but kept the cost of rent and food

A Hard-Knock Life

MANY KIDS MIGHT LIKE TO DREAM about not having to go to school. But the following stories from a Hull House report show that maybe school isn't so bad after all.

Among the occupations in which children are most employed in Chicago, and which most endanger the health, are: The tobacco trade, [which causes] nicotine poisoning . . . frame gilding, in which work a child's fingers are stiffened and throat disease is contracted; button-holing, machine-stitching, and hand-work in tailor or sweat shops, the machine-work producing spinal curvature, and for girls pelvic disorders also, while the unsanitary condition of the shops makes even hand-sewing dangerous; bakeries, where children slowly roast before the ovens; binderies, paper-box and paint factories, where arsenical paper, rotting paste, and the poison of the paints are injurious; boiler-plate works, cutlery works, and metal-stamping works, where the dust produces lung disease. . . .

In a factory where accidents are of almost daily occurrence among the children employed, we are told, "They never get hurt till they get careless." This is no doubt true; but if it be offered as an excuse for the mutilation of children, it is an aggravation of, rather than an excuse for, the crime against the child. To be care-free is one of the prerogatives of childhood.

—from Hull House Maps and Papers (1895)

George Mortimer Pullman (1831–1897).

the same. That turned out to be a costly mistake. Enraged Pullman workers went on strike, protesting that while they were being financially squeezed, the company's owner and stockholders were still making profits.

Labor leader Eugene Debs came to Illinois to lend the support of the American Railway Union. When Pullman ignored their demands, ARU members boycotted all handling of Pullman cars. The boycott brought rail traffic to a nationwide standstill. As the strike wore on, tensions grew. Mobs sympathetic with the Pullman strikers vandalized rail cars. Federal troops were called in. Despite Debs' pleas for calm, the confrontations continued and eventually resulted in a violent clash. On July 7 federal troops shot at rioting mobs, killing 4 and wounding 20.

The strike largely failed, but Pullman didn't live long to enjoy his partial victory. When Pullman died in 1897, his family feared that union sympathizers might try to dig up his grave. To prevent this from happening his family sealed his coffin with steel rails and concrete. In the following year federal courts decided that a private company could not own a town. The Pullman Company was forced to sell its apartments, hotel, and all other properties that were unrelated to the production of their railcars. Now that the company no longer controlled the rents paid by workers, it was no longer a source of disagreement. The Pullman Company continued to grow throughout most of the 20th century.

URBAN JUNGLE

Although it was obviously bad to be unemployed, working at the Chicago stockyards was no treat either. Of the many accounts of life in the slaughterhouses, none is more vivid and disturbing than Upton Sinclair's novel, *The Jungle*. It tells the story of Jurgis Rudkus, a healthy young man living in Lithuania. Hearing legends of wealth and opportunity in the New World, he decides "to go to America and marry, and be a rich man in the bargain."

When Jurgis and his family arrive in America, they know only one word in English: Chicago. Repeating it to anyone who bothers to listen, they are directed to the appropriate train platforms, eventually arriving in Chicago. Once there, they are shocked by the sights, smells, and prices of Chicago. Sinclair wrote, "Down every side street they could see, it was the same—never a hill and never a hollow, but always the

Kipling on Chicago

STRANGE AS IT MAY SOUND, a visit to the stockyards was a popular tourist attraction at the turn of the century. But like many Chicago tourists, English novelist Rudyard Kipling was horrified by the experience.

Twelve men stood in two lines—six a-side. Between them and overhead ran the railway of death. . . . [Pigs] were flicked persuasively, a few at a time, into a smaller chamber, and there a man fixed tackle on their hinder legs so that they rose in the air suspended from the railway of death. Oh! it was then they shrieked and called on their mothers and made promises of amendment, till the tackle-man punted them in their backs, and they slid head down into a brick-floored passage, very like a big kitchen sink that was blood-red. There awaited them a red man with a knife which he passed jauntily through their throats, and the full-voiced shriek became a sputter, and then a fall as of heavy tropical rain.

—from *As Others See Chicago* (1933), compiled by Bessie Louise Pierce

same endless vista of ugly and dirty little wooden buildings. . . . Here and there would be a great factory, a dingy building with innumerable windows in it, and immense volumes of smoke pouring from the chimneys, darkening the air above and making filthy the earth beneath."

Walking about their new neighborhood they see swarms of children playing in the "stinking green water" that runs in the streets. There are so many children present that "you thought there must be a school just out." Only later did they learn that "there was no school" for these children.

Exploring the city, Jurgis and his group meet a Lithuanian who had been living in Chicago for some time. At first they feel lucky to meet a person who "could tell them what to do." But their joy soon turns to despair when they learn the harsh realities of immigrant life in America. In Chicago, they are horrified to learn "the poor man was almost as poor as in any other corner of the earth." Or poorer. The only shelter they can afford is in a filthy boardinghouse overcrowded with people, chickens, rats, and insects. "And so there vanished in a night all the wonderful dreams of wealth that had been haunting Jurgis."

Despite all this, Jurgis is still impressed by Chicago. "It all seemed a dream of wonder,

After visiting the Union Stock Yards, a tourist might send postcards like these to friends and family.
COURTESY OF KENAN HEISE

93

with its tale of human energy, of things being done, of employment for thousands upon thousands of men, of opportunity and freedom, of life and love and joy."

Jurgis's first job is to "shovel guts" that fall on the slaughterhouse floor after the

The first edition of *The Jungle*, published in 1906.
COURTESY OF KENAN HEISE

cow's stomach is sliced open. Pushing them through a hole in the floor, he has to be careful not to fall through it himself. He also has to watch out for the many razor-sharp knives being wielded by other workers. In the winter, the unheated rooms are just as cold as the outdoors. "On the killing beds, you were apt to be covered with blood, and it would freeze solid" against their clothes and skin. With their hands numb from the cold, "of course there would be accidents."

With his new job Jurgis is just barely making enough to get by. But then the family is cheated by a real estate agent and Jurgis gets injured on the job and can no longer work. The children are forced to find jobs. One works in a factory, where "hour after hour, day after day, year after year, it was fated that he should stand upon a certain square foot of floor from seven in the morning until noon, and again from half-past twelve till half-past five." His pay for this miserable job is three dollars a week.

The younger kids "were sent out to make their way to the city and learn to sell newspapers." This job has more freedom, but very long hours with very little pay. "Leaving home at four o'clock in the morning, and running about the streets, first with morning papers and then with

evening, they might come home late at night with twenty or thirty cents apiece."

The Jungle exposed the horrors of life in Chicago's stockyards, but the book did not have the effect that the author, Upton Sinclair, hoped for. He hoped his book would improve working conditions and wages for workers. Instead, by showing how the packing houses sold spoiled meat and unsafe animal parts to the public, the book led the government to pass new food safety laws. Appalled by what he read in *The Jungle*, President Theodore Roosevelt was said to have been so disgusted that he tossed his breakfast sausages out of a window.

Summing up his disappointment, Sinclair later remarked, "I aimed at the public's heart and by accident I hit it in the stomach."

A GENUINE REFUGE

One other person who recognized the dangers of poverty was Jane Addams. Addams not only wrote about the problems she saw, she chose to live among the impoverished and make daily practical improvements to her new neighborhood.

Addams' father was a successful business-man and an Illinois state legislator, so she grew up in the comfort of the upper-middle class. But Addams found it difficult to enjoy the privileges of money and social position while so many around her suffered from poverty and hunger.

On a trip to England, Addams had an experience that changed her life. She visited a settlement house called Toynbee Hall in London. A settlement house is a place where more fortunate members of society can live among the poor in order to help them improve their lives.

In 1889 Jane Addams and her friend, Ellen Gates Starr, moved into an old house in a poor section of the West Side of Chicago. "In our enthusiasm over 'settling,'" she later recalled, "the first night we forgot not only to lock but to close a side door opening on Polk Street." Luckily, nothing happened, which the ladies took as "a fine illustration of the honesty and kindliness of our new neighbors."

The neighborhood was a melting pot of poor immigrants from all over the world, including Germans, Irish, Italians, Poles, Russians, and Jewish people from various countries. In a book called *Twenty Years at Hull House*, Jane Addams described the neighborhood this way:

"The streets are inexpressibly dirty, the number of schools inadequate, sanitary legislation unenforced, the street lighting bad, the paving miserable and altogether lacking in the alleys and smaller streets, and the stables foul beyond description. Hundreds of houses are unconnected with the street sewer. . . . Many houses have no water supply save the faucet in the back yard, [and] there are no fire escapes."

Addams and Starr named their settlement house at 800 South Halsted Street after the original owner of the home, "one of Chicago's pioneer citizens, Mr. Charles J. Hull." They hoped that Hull House would provide their neighbors with "a genuine refuge" from the effects of poverty. From the very beginning, Jane Addams was convinced that the best way to help her neighbors was to feed not only their bodies but their minds and souls, too. In addition to teaching about nutrition and health, she also helped people learn new skills to find better jobs. Hull House ran a kindergarten and after-school clubs for children. They even provided reading groups and sponsored lectures on art and music.

More importantly, residents also did research on living conditions in the area. In some cases their efforts led to new laws and policies designed to help improve health and education, housing and working conditions in the neighborhood. For example, Hull House published a report on sweatshops and child labor that resulted in state laws that forbade

Jane Addams (1860–1935).

Children at Hull House in the 1890s.

children under 14 to work and also limited the number of hours that older children and women could work in a given week.

To this day the Jane Addams Hull House Association continues to provide social services throughout the city of Chicago, including literacy training, early childhood development, and after-school care programs. Hull House also provides services and resources to senior citizens as well as to fledgling small businesses.

Hull House wasn't the only institution helping out Chicago's needy. The Central Relief Association had been around since 1857. In 1871 it was put in charge of distributing $5 million in donations for victims of the Great Chicago Fire. Renamed the Bureau of Charities in 1894, the organization provided a range of services to the unemployed, the working poor, the sick, the elderly, and the homeless.

Another source of charity may come as a surprise: free lunches served at saloons. Even though some people complained about the large number of establishments serving alcoholic drinks to poor workers, even the most bitter critics of tavern owners had to admit that without them countless Chicagoans would have starved. As many as half of the estimated 6,000 to 7,000 taverns in Chicago were serving free lunches to

Trace Your Family History

Other than descendants of Native American tribes, everybody who lives in Chicago is either an immigrant or the descendant of an immigrant. Because Chicago is a fairly young city, most Chicagoans can trace their family history back to the point when their first ancestor moved here.

Make a photocopy of the family tree at right or draw one of your own. Fill in as many blanks as you can. Ask your parents for help filling in the names of your grandparents, great-grandparents, and so on. Talk to other relatives—aunts, uncles, grandparents, and so on—collecting as much information as you can. Were you able to identify which members of your family were first generation immigrants to Chicago or to America?

If not, do some research at home or at the library. The best online resource is www.ancestry.com. The Newberry Library in Chicago is an especially good place to do genealogy research. See www.newberry.org/genealogy/collections.html.

It might help to find newspaper obituaries for deceased relatives. Search the paper's archives, using the deceased's full name, date of birth, and date of death. You can also consult the Cook County Birth Index, 1871–1916, or the Cook County Death Index, 1871–1916. It also helps to try to find marriage records, as these will contain information about parents and siblings.

You may also want to consult the following books:

Finding Your Chicago Ancestors: A Beginner's Guide to Family History in the City and Cook County by Grace DuMelle (Lake Claremont Press, 2005)

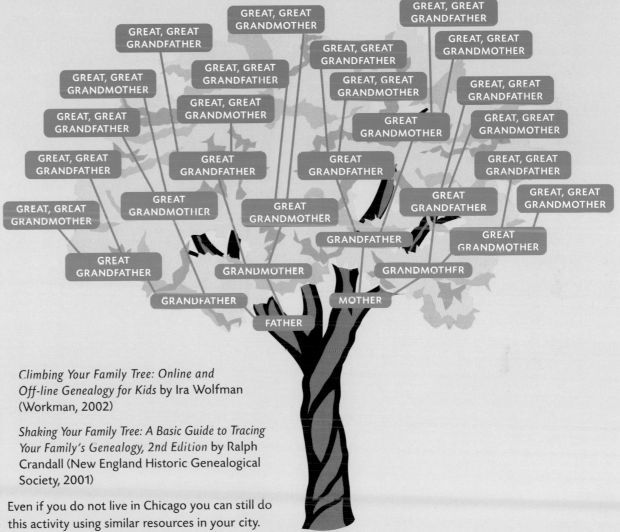

Climbing Your Family Tree: Online and Off-line Genealogy for Kids by Ira Wolfman (Workman, 2002)

Shaking Your Family Tree: A Basic Guide to Tracing Your Family's Genealogy, 2nd Edition by Ralph Crandall (New England Historic Genealogical Society, 2001)

Even if you do not live in Chicago you can still do this activity using similar resources in your city.

poor and out-of-work Chicagoans. That works out to about 60,000 free lunches each day. Other taverns would provide a complimentary lunch to anyone who could afford a nickel beer.

CRIME BEFORE IT GOT ORGANIZED

Crime was always a part of city life, but it seems to have gotten much worse at this time. "During the last two months of 1905 and the first two months of 1906," said Herbert Asbury in *The Gem of the Prairie*, "the crime wave reached its crest; the average citizen . . . was probably in greater danger of being robbed and murdered than at any other time in the history of Chicago."

The dangers of the city were reflected in the colorful nicknames given to neighborhoods, like Hell's Half-Acre, Dead Man's Alley, the Bad Lands, Satan's Mile, Little Hell, Hairtrigger Block, and Bucket of Blood. The small police force was no match for the city's criminal element. "With nothing to stop them," writes Asbury, "bands of thugs and hoodlums prowled the streets from dusk to dawn. They robbed every pedestrian they encountered, and many of these holdups were remarkable for brutality."

The city had its share of crooks and low-lifes, like saloon owner Mickey Finn. The specialty of the house was called the Mickey Finn Special, a drink mixed with poisonous knockout drops. Any customer who ordered a Mickey Finn Special would pass out soon after drinking it. He or she was then dragged into a back room, stripped, and robbed before being thrown into the back alley.

One of the most senseless Chicago crime waves at the turn of the century was perpetrated by a gang of young hoodlums who called themselves the Automatic Trio. In the summer of 1903 Gustave Marx, Harvey Van Dine, and Peter Neidermeyer—all of them under the age of 24—went on a violent crime spree. In a series of holdups the gang killed eight people, including two detectives.

Unfortunately for the Automatic Trio, they were just as dumb as they were vicious. They freely spent the stolen money in Chicago's saloons and gambling halls. Coming from poor families and never holding jobs, they soon became suspects in the string of holdups. They also liked to talk about their exploits. Van Dine bragged about how he once killed a saloon owner named Benjamin C. LaGross and a customer named Adolph Johnson in one robbery.

"I let 'em have both guns at once and Johnson fell, hit in the stomach. LaGross

got to the door and I gave him another shot. He dropped in the doorway. Then I went home. I slept fine. We got eight dollars out of that haul. We killed two men—four dollars apiece."

The police arrested Marx first, at a saloon on the city's North Side. Killing one of the cops during his arrest, Marx later complained, "You can't do anything to me. I only shot a cop! Anybody's got a right to shoot a cop!"

The others were quickly rounded up after Marx tattled on his pals and even showed police where to find the gang's hideout. But the Automatic Trio's biggest mistake was taking so much pride in their crimes. Playing up to the newspapers and the public at their carnival-like trial all but guaranteed them a date with the gallows. All three were hung at the Cook County Jail on April 22, 1904.

Not all the thugs in this era of Chicago crime were men. A gang of ruthless women held up hundreds of victims on Chicago's South Side in the 1890s. Flossie Moore, Emma Ford, Pearl Smith, and Mary White were some of the strongest and most violent women to ever prey upon victims in the city of Chicago. "They usually worked in pairs," writes Asbury, "and were armed with revolvers, razors, brass knuckles, knives, and sawed-off baseball bats; one of their favorite tricks, if a victim didn't raise his hands quick enough to suit them, was to slash him across the knuckles with a razor."

Mary White must have done something to earn the nickname the Strangler. Of Emma Ford, one detective said that "she would never submit to arrest, except at the point of a revolver. No two men on the police force were strong enough to handle her, and she was dreaded by all of them." One by one, these women were rounded up and brought to justice by a detective named Clifton Wooldridge.

Wooldridge was not only an effective police officer, but also one of the most colorful characters in the history of the Chicago police. He once jumped onto the shoulders of a thief he arrested and rode him like a pony to the police station. And Wooldridge would often hide his identity with one of the 75 disguises he used for undercover work.

HOMEGROWN CLASSICS

Depending on your situation, Chicago could be a city of wonders and joys or a city of misery and dread. Some of the city's unlucky residents no doubt tried to escape their real-life problems through the world

of imagination. In their dreams, they might journey to mysterious lands and meet fantastical characters. At least two young Chicagoans did just that, trading average jobs for writing careers. In the process they created unforgettable tales that would fascinate readers and moviegoers the world over.

A young Chicago newspaper reporter and part-time traveling salesman, L. Frank Baum was fond of telling stories to his children. And he always took notes of the people he met and the things he saw on his travels. Eventually he wrote his stories down and found a publisher. Baum's first books were *Mother Goose in Prose* and *Father Goose, His Book*, the second of which became a national bestseller. But today he's best known for his tale of munchkins, a yellow-brick road, a talking scarecrow, wicked witches, and flying monkeys.

The Wonderful Wizard of Oz became Baum's second-straight bestselling children's book in 1900. The story of Dorothy Gale and Toto made Baum famous and secured his reputation as a talented children's-book author. Later, Baum helped adapt his book to a musical stage production called *The Wizard of Oz*, which was a smash hit on Broadway and in a traveling production. In 1925 it was made into a silent film, and

The first edition of *The Wonderful Wizard of Oz*.
LIBRARY OF CONGRESS, RARE BOOK & SPECIAL COLLECTIONS DIVISION

in 1939 MGM adapted the story into the famous movie starring Judy Garland.

Another world-famous tale of adventure in a faraway land was written by Chicagoan Edgar Rice Burroughs. As a young man Burroughs had tried to make a living in a variety of jobs. He went from being a railway policeman, to a door-to-door salesman, to a clerk at Sears, Roebuck & Company. His last job was as a sales manager for a company that made pencil sharpeners. One of his duties for this last job was to leaf through story magazines to make sure that

The first edition of *The Return of Tarzan.*

COURTESY OF KENAN HEISE

the advertisements his company purchased actually appeared where they were supposed to. Naturally, he eventually began reading the stories too.

"If people were paid for writing rot such as I read in some of those magazines," Burroughs later claimed, "I could write stories just as rotten." Rotten or not, he managed to sell a couple of minor stories to magazines before hitting the jackpot with "Tarzan of the Apes," which was published in the October 1912 edition of *All-Story* magazine. The story was published as a book in 1914 and made into a silent movie in 1918. The 1932 talking version starring Johnny Weissmuller as Tarzan gained the greatest fame and made Burroughs a household name.

Chicagoans could also find relief from their cares at two of the world's first modern-style amusement parks. Riverview Park opened in 1904, followed by the White City amusement park, which opened in 1905. At Riverview, Chicagoans could ride the world's first suspended roller coaster (1908) and the first parachute ride (1936).

THE OLD BALL GAME

Unfortunately, Chicagoans found few thrills at the ballpark during this era. The Chicago White Stockings baseball team that had been so successful in the late 1880s went through a major losing streak starting in the 1890s. They not only lost their winning ways but their identity, too. When long-time star and manager Adrian "Cap" Anson was fired in 1898 the team came to be known as the Orphans. They had dismal seasons for the next four years. During this period the team was known by a variety of names, including the Colts, the Black Stockings, the Rainmakers, the Cowboys, and the Rough Riders.

In 1900 a new baseball team arrived in Chicago. Charles Comiskey brought his minor league team from St. Paul, Minnesota, down to Chicago to become part of the new American League. In its first act of rivalry against Chicago's National League team, Comiskey's team swiped the now-unused White Stockings name. On opening day of the 1901 season the team name was officially shortened to White Sox. The White Sox won their league championship in their first two years of existence.

In 1902 Chicago's many-named National League team hired a new manager, Frank Selee, to lead the young squad now dubbed the Cubs by sportswriters. Thankfully, that name, which the team officially adopted in 1907, has stuck now for the last 100 years. Under Selee the Cubs had winning seasons through 1908.

One of Selee's more effective decisions was to move a backup catcher by the name of Frank Chance to the first base position. With Joe Tinker at shortstop and Johnny Evers at second base, this made possible the world-famous double-play combination of Tinker to Evers to Chance.

In 1906, the Cubs and White Sox both put together incredible seasons, each winning their league pennant. That meant that the two Chicago ball clubs would meet in the World Series—the first and last time this has happened. With a record of 116–36 the Cubs were highly favored to win the "Trolley Series" against a White Sox squad (93–58) that was strong in pitching and fielding but weak in hitting. Known as the "Hitless Wonders," the White Sox team batting average was just .230 (lowest in the American League), compared to the .262 team batting average for the Cubs (highest in the National League).

The White Sox not only outpitched the Cubs, they outhit them too, winning the 1906 World Series 4–2. The Cubs players felt bad enough to have lost to the underdog White Sox. Even worse, many of them had bet their expected postseason winnings on their team to win and now had to come up with the cash.

The Sox faltered in the next two years, while the Cubs surged back, winning the

Tinker to Evers to Chance

IN 1910, NEW YORK WRITER Franklin Pierce Adams penned baseball's most famous poem, "Baseball's Sad Lexicon." As a fan of the Cubs' rival team the New York Giants, Adams knew all too well how discouraging it was to go up against the game's most effective double-play combination of Cubs shortstop Joe Tinker to second baseman Johnny Evers to first baseman Frank Chance: Tinker to Evers to Chance.

Joe Tinker (1880–1948), John Evers (1881–1947), and Frank Chance (1877–1924).
AUTHOR'S COLLECTION

BASEBALL'S SAD LEXICON

These are the saddest of all possible words:

"Tinker to Evers to Chance."

Trio of Bear-cubs, fleeter than birds,

Tinker to Evers to Chance.

Ruthlessly pricking our gonfalon bubble,

Making a Giant hit into a double—

Words that are weighty with nothing but trouble:

"Tinker to Evers to Chance."

Game 5 of the 1906 World Series, the first and last time the Cubs and White Sox squared off in the World Series.

World Series in 1907 and 1908. They haven't won it since. But no matter how bad things got for Chicago's sports teams, at least it was never a matter of life and death.

FIRE AND WATER

Tragically, there have been times in Chicago's history when people seeking entertainment have put their very lives at risk. Chicago's deadliest fire took place at a musical theater production. Chicago's deadliest disaster of any kind occurred on a pleasure cruise.

Just as Peshtigo's much deadlier 1871 fire was overshadowed by the Great Chicago Fire, the Iroquois Theater Fire is widely overlooked today, even though it claimed many more lives than the Chicago Fire. On the evening of December 30, 1903, theatergoers streamed through the doors of the Iroquois Theater, which had opened just one month earlier. Described by owners as "absolutely fireproof" and touted by the *Chicago Tribune* as "one of the splendid theaters of the world," the Iroquois Theater was a popular place to see a musical.

The show being performed that evening was *Mr. Bluebeard*, a musical comedy

starring local favorite Eddie Foy. During the second act sparks from a faulty spotlight ignited a nearby curtain. In minutes, the stage was engulfed in flames and smoke. Panic-stricken patrons stampeded toward the exits. In all, 602 people (150 of them children) died from burns, smoke inhalation, and suffocation due to trampling.

An investigation found that the building's owners had taken shortcuts in order to open their theater on schedule. Fire hazards had been overlooked, including doors that opened inward instead of outward. But the owners were never convicted of manslaughter and few of the victims and their families ever received any compensation.

As bad as the Iroquois Theater fire was, it was not Chicago's most deadly disaster. On July 14, 1915, the Western Electric company arranged a boat excursion for its employees. Several ships, including a steamer called the *Eastland*, were to take the employees from downtown Chicago to Michigan City, Indiana. But the vessel never got out of the Chicago River. In fact, it didn't get but a few feet from shore.

The poorly designed boat was top-heavy, making it unstable. With 2,500 passengers aboard, the boat tipped dangerously from side to side. After one especially big lurch, nervous passengers instinctively rushed to

Crowds gather to look at the overturned *Eastland*, several days after the disaster. The boat is seen here floating on its side, with the deck facing the camera.

the opposite side, causing the entire boat to flip over. Many of the passengers were tossed overboard or trapped belowdecks. Some that were above decks were able to swim to safety or were plucked from the water by rescuers. Those trapped below fared much worse. The *Eastland* disaster resulted in the deaths of 844 people.

It was later learned that owners of the *Eastland* were aware of the boat's stability problems. The boat had almost capsized once before in 1904. The owners made several changes to the vessel to try to make it more stable. They also added more lifeboats on the ship's deck, making the vessel even more top-heavy.

8

Turning Point

BERTHA HONORÉ PALMER never did anything on a small scale—in life or in death. At the peak of her fame she hosted grand balls at the North Side mansion built by her tycoon husband, Potter Palmer. With her fine taste in art, Bertha decorated the walls of the Palmer home with paintings by Impressionist painters, such as Frenchmen Claude Monet and Pierre Auguste Renoir, as well as the American Mary Cassatt. She even took her favorite paintings with her whenever she traveled the world.

Time Line

1918 Bertha Honoré Palmer dies; Cubs win pennant but lose World Series; over 10,000 deaths related to pulmonary diseases, many caused by flu epidemic; World War I ends

1919 Steel strike; White Sox throw World Series in Black Sox Scandal; Great Migration in full swing; race riots sparked by squabble over beach access

1920 Bears football team inaugurated (as Decatur Staleys)

1921 Al Capone moves to Chicago from New York, where he was wanted by the police for murder

1922 Jazz trumpeter Louis Armstrong moves to Chicago from New Orleans

1923 Eight-hour workday established for steelworkers

1924 Nathan Leopold Jr. and Richard Loeb murder Bobby Franks

1925 Chicago Cardinals win NFL Championship

In the early 1900s the corner of State and Madison was considered by many to be the world's busiest intersection.
COURTESY OF KENAN HEISE

This early 1900s photograph, taken near the corner of Foster and Kedzie Avenues, shows that much of Chicago's outer reaches were yet to be developed.

Bertha Palmer was the closest thing Chicago ever had to royalty. She entertained visiting kings, queens, presidents, and prime ministers, as well as the cream of Chicago society. She arranged events for artists, writers, and intellectuals from around the world. Bertha Honoré Palmer was the picture of grace, beauty, and intelligence. As mentioned previously, she served as the chairperson of the Board of Lady Managers during the 1893 World's Columbian Exposition. She traveled the world. She was also a wise businessperson, who doubled the size of her family's fortune after her husband's death. She even had a variety of rose named after her.

On May 5, 1918, Bertha Honoré Palmer died at her vacation home in Osprey, Florida. Her body was returned to Chicago by train. Thousands of curious onlookers lined Lake Shore Drive to witness the funeral procession from the Palmer mansion to Graceland Cemetery. She was buried beside her husband, Potter, who had died 16 years earlier.

Bertha Palmer's death marked the end of an era. Chicago's age of aristocracy had come to an end. The incredibly rich captains of industry, the benefactors of museums, the wearers of tuxedos, the riders of carriages—they were all gone now. Marshall Field, Cyrus McCormick, George Pullman,

William B. Ogden, Augustus Swift, and Philip Armour were only memories.

The year 1919 could have been so good for Chicago and the world. World War I was over. The U.S. Congress passed two important amendments: The 18th Amendment (also known as Prohibition) outlawed the manufacture and sale of alcoholic beverages. The 19th Amendment gave women the right to vote. Each one inspired hope that progress was being made—that life would be better in the future.

Some of the soldiers returning from military service in WWI were professional baseball players, including many of the stars that had helped the White Sox win the 1917 World Series. With Urban "Red" Faber, Oscar "Happy" Felsch, Charles August "Swede" Risberg, Claude "Lefty" Williams, and "Shoeless" Joe Jackson back in Sox uniforms, hopes were especially high for a 1919 World Series Championship.

Hopes were high on the North Side, too. The Chicago Cubs had won the National League pennant in the war-shortened season of 1918. They ended up losing the World Series to the Boston Red Sox and a young pitcher named George Herman "Babe" Ruth. Oddly, during the 1918 World Series the Cubs played their home games in Comiskey Park. The home of the Chicago White Sox was larger than Wrigley Field and could accommodate more spectators.

But there were storm clouds on the horizon too. A worldwide outbreak of Spanish flu hit Chicago hard. Before it ended, 20,000 Chicagoans would die in the epidemic that claimed 50 million victims worldwide. Troop movements in the world war had made it easier for the flu bug to spread from country to country and across oceans. And so did the ever-improving transportation networks made up of ocean liners and railways. With the opening of the first international airline in 1919, airplanes would only make it easier to spread diseases.

THE GREAT MIGRATION

The war was also one of the factors that encouraged large numbers of southern blacks to move north. There were several reasons for this. Up north, there were more jobs and higher wages than in the South. When World War I started in 1914, northern factories needed to produce more materials to fill overseas orders. At the same time, there were fewer workers available. With the hostilities in Europe, the United States closed off its borders to foreign immigration, so there were fewer newcomers to fill all the open job positions. The labor short-age got even worse when the United States entered the war. In 1917 the United States was sending many of its able-bodied young men off to war. So who was going to work in Chicago's factories?

There were other reasons why African Americans wanted to leave the South. Things hadn't gotten much better for them in the 50 years since slavery ended. Jim Crow laws made it legal to discriminate

Cultural Migration

IN ADDITION TO workers, northern cities also attracted African American musicians, artists, and writers. Louis "Satchmo" Armstrong moved from New Orleans to Chicago in 1922 to join the Joe Oliver Creole Jazz Band, which played at South Side clubs. Richard Wright, an aspiring writer, moved from Jackson, Mississippi, to Memphis, Tennessee, in 1925 and then to Chicago in 1927. While working at the post office, Wright wrote short stories and began working on his novel, *Native Son*, which was published in 1940.

Between 1916 and 1919 about 50,000 African Americans moved north seeking opportunities and freedoms they lacked down south. Many others, like the men pictured here, also enlisted to serve in the military during World War I.

NATIONAL ARCHIVES, ARC ID: 533614

against African Americans. As a result southern blacks didn't have fair and equal access to public resources, such as schools, parks, and libraries. They were not allowed to vote in government elections. And there were many examples of blacks being cheated out of property by whites. The criminal court system also favored whites, so it usually didn't do any good for a black man to take a white man to court.

In fact, southern blacks feared to stand up for their rights, because doing so could get them killed. Lynchings—public murders intended to intimidate African Americans—were carried out for even small offenses, such as talking back to a white man or even just speaking to a white woman. The lack of freedoms and the threat of violence were enough to make many blacks want to leave.

If southern blacks needed any extra encouragement to move north, they found it in articles printed in the *Chicago Defender*, a newspaper produced especially for an African American audience. Though published in Chicago, the *Defender* was mailed to subscribers all over the country. Southern blacks reading the *Defender* would discover stories of opportunity and freedom in Chicago, stories that captured their imagination and made them believe that in the North they too could live the American dream.

Barnstormin' Bessie

ONE OF THE MORE INTERESTING STORIES of African Americans who moved to Chicago in the Great Migration was Bessie Coleman. At a time when U.S. flight schools were generally off-limits to women and African Americans, Coleman learned to speak French and learned how to fly airplanes in France. The first female African American pilot, Coleman flew from town to town on a promotional tour sponsored by the *Chicago Defender* newspaper. In 1926 Coleman died when her plane crashed in Jacksonville, Florida. The city of Chicago later named a street at O'Hare International Airport in her honor.

Beginning in 1916, the *Defender*'s readers also learned about the opportunities available in northern cities, especially in Chicago. The *Defender* published practical information, such as job listings. The Chicago Urban League also helped black migrants find jobs and housing.

Thanks to the growing network of U.S. railroads, it was easier than ever to travel from the South to the North. As the nation's railway hub and as a center for manufacturing, Chicago was a popular destination in what has been called the Great Migration. From 1916 to 1970 about half a million African Americans moved to Chicago. In that time the city's African American population rose from two percent to about one-third of Chicagoans. Blacks moved north from southern states like Mississippi, Alabama, and Louisiana, following jobs and fleeing discrimination. Unfortunately, they found more discrimination than jobs waiting for them in big northern cities.

As long as the war was going on, there were jobs to be had in Chicago. But when white soldiers came home after the war, they got their jobs back and African Americans were out of luck. It didn't help that production dipped as the need for war materials no longer existed. Competition over jobs and housing made relations between whites and blacks uneasy.

In the South, African Americans had been the victims of institutionalized racism, formal laws that said, "You can't go here or do that." Even though the restrictions were less obvious in the North, attitudes and prejudices made it hard for blacks to find good jobs and adequate housing. Many African Americans bunched together in the same neighborhoods, where there was a lack of opportunity. Unemployment and poor education were factors contributing to the poverty and crime that turned some of these neighborhoods into slums, much like the ghettos made up of Italians, Irish, Polish, and Slavs 20 to 40 years earlier.

FROM AMERICAN DREAM TO AMERICAN NIGHTMARE

Racial tensions exploded in a dramatic outbreak of racial violence in 1919. Although there were no "Whites Only" signs, everybody knew that there was an invisible line that separated the "white beach" north of 29th Street and the "black beach" south of 29th Street. On July 27, 1919, a raft carrying a group of African American teenagers drifted across the line. A white man hurled rocks at the teens from the beach. At least one rock struck Eugene Williams, who fell into the water. Unable to swim, the black teenager drowned. A white police officer on the scene not only failed to arrest the white assailant but also did nothing to assist Williams.

Winged Foot Blimp Disaster

ON JULY 21, 1919, a disaster of another sort occurred. A group of passengers embarked on a pleasure cruise aboard the gas-filled blimp called the Winged Foot. The trip from Grant Park to the White City Amusement Park was interrupted when the craft caught fire and plunged through the glass skylight of the Illinois Trust & Savings Bank. Three passengers and 10 employees working at the bank died. Burning fuel and falling debris injured another 27 employees.

Here's how a *Chicago Tribune* reporter described the events:

Racial feeling, which had been on a par with the weather during the day took fire shortly after 5 o'clock when white bathers at the Twenty-ninth street improvised beach saw a colored boy on a raft, paddling into what they termed "white" territory.

A snarl of protest went up from the whites and soon a volley of rocks and stones were sent in his direction. One rock, said to have been thrown by George Stauber of 2904 Cottage Grove avenue, struck the lad and he toppled into the water.

Cop Refuses to Interfere
Colored Men who were present attempted to go to his rescue, but they were kept back by the whites, it is said. Colored men and women, it is alleged, asked

Policeman Dan Callahan of the Cottage Grove station to arrest Stauber, but he is said to have refused.

Then, indignant at the conduct of the policeman, the Negroes set upon Stauber and commenced to pommel him. The whites came to his rescue and then the battle royal was on. Fists flew and rocks were hurled. Bathers from the colored Twenty-fifth street beach were attracted to the scene of the battling and aided their comrades in driving the whites into the water.

Negroes Chase Policeman
Then they turned on Policeman Callahan and drove him down Twenty-ninth street. . . .

Whites Arm Selves
News of the afternoon doings had spread through all parts of the South Side by nightfall, and whites stood at all prominent corners ready to avenge the beatings their brethren had received. Along Halsted and State streets they were armed with clubs, and every Negro who appeared was pommeled.

Violence continued over the next few days with beatings, stabbings, and shootings of both whites and blacks. On July 28 Mayor William Hale Thompson called on the governor of Illinois to provide a regiment of the Illinois National Guard to quell the violence.

Although the riots obviously marked a new low point in Chicago race relations, there were examples of cooperation and compassion across the races. There was one account of a group of African American nurses working at Provident Hospital coming to the aid of the white superintendent who was being threatened by African Americans. Most of the black policemen and also military veterans of World War I assisted the mostly white police in trying to enforce the law and bring peace back to the city. This cooperation was all the more amazing considering the amounts of discrimination black police officers and military personnel faced at the time.

When it was over, the riots had claimed the lives of 23 African Americans and

The Illinois National Guard was called in to end the race riots of 1919. Here they question an African American man.

15 whites. The race riots of 1919 remain one of the most embarrassing chapters in Chicago's racial history.

CON GAMES

Chicagoans were much in need of distraction from the riots and the flu epidemic. Fortunately the White Sox provided the city with many thrills and much pride all summer long. The Sox won the American League pennant with a record of 88–52. Veteran pitcher Eddie Cicotte went 29–7, and the team led the league in batting average, runs scored, hits, and stolen bases.

Almost everyone expected the heavily favored White Sox to win the World Series against the Cincinnati Reds. But for some reason, as the series started, the gambling odds were about even. Why were so many people betting on the Reds? Did the professional gamblers know something that the average fan didn't? They sure did. The White Sox players had secretly arranged to lose the World Series on purpose in return for secret payoffs from gamblers. That way the gamblers—not to mention the players— could place large bets on the Reds to win.

But why would baseball players do such a thing? Didn't they have any personal pride? Didn't winning mean more than money?

White Sox pitching ace Eddie Cicotte (1884–1969) was a key member of the Black Sox conspirators.

From Player to Manager to Owner

BEFORE HE BECAME the penny-pinching owner of the Chicago White Sox, Charles Comiskey was a player and then a manager. As a player he pioneered now-common baseball strategies like the double play and backing up throws. He played first base for the St. Louis Browns team that beat the Chicago White Stockings (future Cubs) in the 1886 World Series.

Ironically, he left the Browns in 1890 to join the short-lived Players League, which was formed in protest against owners who paid their players too little. Taking a pay cut in his new role as a team manager, Comiskey stated, "I couldn't do anything else and still play square with the boys."

Comiskey was also famous for his competitive temper. There's a legend about how one night he was dining at a fancy restaurant. Comiskey objected when the waiter brought him a lobster with only one claw. "It's not unusual for a lobster to lose a claw when fighting with another lobster," the waiter explained. Comiskey shoved the plate at the waiter and snorted, "Bring me the winner."

Back then, before athletes were paid outrageously large amounts of money to play games, things were different. There was no such thing as a free agent. A rule called the reserve clause meant that owners could pay their players whatever they wanted. Players had to take it or leave it because other owners were forbidden to use a player who refused a job with another team.

The owner of the White Sox, Charles Comiskey, was a notorious cheapskate, at least when it came to his players. He paid his top talent less than half of what average players made on other teams. He also made the players wash their own uniforms after games, rather than pay to have them laundered. Even more infuriating, Comiskey could be very generous to others, like members of the press. Even though he shortchanged his players, on game days Comiskey always laid out a lavish spread of food and drinks for reporters.

The last straw for first baseman Chick Gandil came during the 1919 season. The players demanded that their war-era salaries be raised now that postwar attendance had rebounded. But Comiskey refused to even discuss the matter. Gandil made arrangements with a gambling friend of his to lose the World Series, promising to round up seven co-conspirators. Pitcher Eddie Cicotte was an obvious choice. As the best pitcher on the team, Cicotte was crucial to a fix. He was also one of the most disgruntled players. When he complained to Comiskey earlier in the season about his low salary, Comiskey promised to pay Cicotte a bonus if the right hander won 30 games. But after Cicotte reached 29 wins, Comiskey instructed his manager, William "Kid" Gleason, to bench Cicotte for the remainder of the season. Cicotte would make Comiskey pay one way or another.

Cicotte and "Lefty" Williams each purposely lost the first two World Series games they pitched. Dickie Kerr, who was not in on the fix, won both of his two outings. After game six the Reds were leading the nine-game series, 4–2. They needed just one more victory to win the series. This is where it got really interesting. Some of the players were having second thoughts about their role in the fix. The players had only received a fraction of the promised money, and their pride was beginning to make them wonder if it was all worth it.

The gamblers started to get nervous too, and came up with some extra money to seal the deal. But when the Sox won game seven, 4–1, the gamblers decided not to take any more chances. If Williams had any thoughts about trying to win game eight, those plans went out the window the night before. As Williams and his wife left a restaurant, they were approached by a stranger. You better throw the game, the stranger threatened, or something bad might happen to the little lady. Williams pitched horribly the next day, recording only one out and giving up 3 runs in the first inning. Before it was over, the Reds had won the game, 10–1, and the World Series, 5–3.

Rumors of the fix had been swirling around ever since game one. Several newspaper reporters were skeptical about some of the "errors" made on the field. After the series was over, suspicion grew and grew. Comiskey and manager Kid Gleason didn't need any evidence. They knew that the players hadn't played the way they could. But they had no proof, and the following season began under a cloud of doubt.

Late in the 1920 season some gamblers spilled the beans on the fix, and a grand jury conducted an investigation. On September 26, 1920, Shoeless Joe Jackson took the witness stand, admitting his guilt in the affair. On his way out of the courtroom, Jackson was famously confronted by a young boy.

"Say it ain't so, Joe. Say it ain't so."

But there was nothing Jackson could say to comfort the child—or any baseball fan for that matter. The unthinkable had really

Comiskey's Polar Opposite

WHEN LOOKING FOR the model of a real players' owner, look no further than Andrew "Rube" Foster, the player-manager-owner of Chicago's African American baseball team, the Leland Giants. The future Hall of Famer led his team, later renamed the American Giants, to numerous victorious seasons in various African American semipro baseball leagues. Foster was a popular owner, because he made sure his players were paid good wages. He was also a winner. In 1910 the Giants' record was an incredible 123–6. Ten years later Foster put his organizational skills to use in helping to start the Negro National League.

"Shoeless" Joe Jackson (1887–1951).
LIBRARY OF CONGRESS, LC-USZ62-78070

happened. The eight "Black Sox" players, as they came to be known after the scandal, were kicked out of professional baseball for life. To this day they remain ineligible for induction in the Major League Baseball Hall of Fame. In the end the players only received about half of the money gamblers promised to pay them.

BACK WHERE CRIME BELONGS

The baseball diamond may seem like an odd place to find crime. But what else would you expect from a town with Chicago's reputation for bribes, payoffs, illegal gambling, and corruption of all sorts? Years before the Black Sox threw the 1919 World Series, the Chicago underworld had been perfecting the art of organized crime. Small-time con artists and petty thieves gave way to big-time crooks who ran gambling houses, saloons, and bordellos—right beneath the noses of the police and mayor.

It's not that Chicago's mayors were unaware of these activities. Some of them even benefited directly or indirectly from the crime industry, in the form of payoffs and possibly votes. Others merely decided that pursuing these criminals wasn't worth the effort. Still others did their best to root out corruption and shut down illegal operations. In 1907 a reformer named Fred Busse was elected to the mayor's office, beating former mayor Carter H. Harrison II. Harrison, like his Chicago mayor father before him, had a live-and-let-live attitude toward the gambling dens, saloons, and prostitution houses that were able to operate freely under his administration. Instead of trying to put them out of business, Harrison preferred to contain them to isolated neighborhoods.

Like Father, Like Son

CHICAGO HAS HAD two sets of father-son mayors. The first two were both named Carter Harrison, the second two were both named Richard Daley. The Harrison father served as mayor from 1879 to 1887 and again in 1893, the son from 1897 to 1905 and from 1911 to 1915.

The elder Mayor Daley (Richard J.) was elected six straight times. He was Chicago's longest running mayor from 1955 to 1976, when he died in office. After winning reelection in 2007, the younger Mayor Daley (Richard M.) will surpass his father's record, as long as he serves his full sixth term in office.

The most notorious "vice district" in Chicago at the turn of the century was called the Levee, a seedy area located on the near South Side of Chicago. Mobsters such as Big Jim Colosimo and Ike Bloom paid first ward aldermen "Bathhouse" John Coughlin and Michael "Hinky Dink" Kenna to protect their illegal businesses from prosecution and police raids.

"The Chicago Democrats went to the polls for their primary elections on September 15 [1920]. It was a frightening demonstration of the city's political climate. There were several killings, shootings, kidnappings, sluggings, riots, robberies, and a brutal attempt to steal a ballot box— all at the polls."—FROM *EIGHT MEN OUT* (1963) BY ELIOT ASINOF

Mayor Busse was more popular with people like Bertha Palmer and Julius Rosenwald, prominent Chicagoans who fretted over the city's bad reputation. Other Busse supporters were Arthur Burrage Farwell, president of the Chicago Law and Order League, church leaders like evangelist preacher Gipsy Smith, and members of the Women's Christian Temperance Union.

During his term, Mayor Busse and his supporters interested in shutting down crime scored several victories. In 1909 they succeeded in canceling the First Ward Ball. The ball was a wild party thrown every year by Coughlin and Kenna, the so-called "Lords of the Levee," to celebrate another profitable year of corruption. In 1910 Busse created a special Vice Commission to investigate activities in the Levee. The commission published a report that shocked many citizens. As a result, a number of high-profile operations were shuttered.

But reform was short-lived. Harrison was reelected mayor in 1911 with the help of crooked aldermen Kenna and Coughlin, and much of the uproar died down. Harrison served as mayor until 1915, when he was replaced by William Hale Thompson. This new mayor promised to clean up the city once again. During his election victory speech, he declared, "The crooks had better move out of Chicago before I am inaugurated."

But they obviously didn't, and Thompson later proved to be full of hot air. If former mayor Harrison tended to turn a blind eye toward vice and corruption, Big Bill Thompson played deaf, dumb, and blind. Thompson may have been the city's most corrupt mayor. He not only did nothing to stop crime, he personally profited from it. When Thompson died in 1944, authorities found that he had $1.5 million in cash hidden in safe deposit boxes—a lot more than he could have saved on a mayor's salary.

"Big Bill" Thompson (1867–1944), possibly Chicago's most corrupt mayor.
LIBRARY OF CONGRESS, LC-DIG-GGBAIN-19321

HOW THE CITY THAT WORKS WORKED

Mayor Thompson was still alive and kicking in 1919 when Prohibition went into effect. Many reformers hoped Prohibition would help clean up the city. It actually made matters worse. By making it illegal to make and sell liquor, the government unintentionally created a huge money-making opportunity for people who didn't worry too much about following laws. The head gang boss at the time, Big Jim Colosimo, was slow to take advantage of the opportunities. Colosimo's right-hand man, Johnny Torrio, saw his opportunity and took it.

Colosimo was murdered in 1920 at his South Side club by a gunman who many believed acted on orders from Torrio.

Johnny Torrio may have been ruthless, but he also had a good business sense. He knew there was demand for his product— with or without Prohibition—so he set up breweries and made deals with the owners of secret illegal taverns, called speakeasies. He eliminated competitors and hired good employees, such as a promising young New Yorker by the name of Alphonse Capone. Capone started his career in Chicago as a small-time thug. Years later, he would become the king of Chicago's criminal empire.

LEOPOLD AND LOEB

Two of the most notorious names in the history of Chicago crime—Nathan Leopold Jr. and Richard Loeb—had nothing to do with the Chicago mob. Neither one of them even had a criminal record or a colorful nickname. In fact, they seemed like model citizens who came from wealthy and respectable families. And they were highly intelligent young men, graduates of top universities. In the end they were too smart for their own good.

In a twisted experiment Leopold and Loeb decided to see if they could commit the perfect murder—and get away with it. On May 21, 1924, they kidnapped and strangled 14-year-old Bobby Franks, hiding the body in a culvert near Wolf Lake. But the two amateur murderers were not satisfied with a simple murder. Instead, they pretended to make it look like a kidnapping. They sent a note to the Franks' home, saying,

> "As you no doubt know by this time, your son has been kidnapped. Allow us to assure you that he is at present well and safe. You need fear no physical harm for him, provided you live up carefully to the following instructions and to such others as you will receive by future communications. Should you, however, disobey any of our instructions, even slightly, his death will be the penalty."

Police quickly determined that the letter had been typed on an Underwood typewriter by someone with an easy command of the English language. In other words, not by your average kidnapper.

By the time the note was received at the Franks' home, however, the boy's body had already been found and identified. The police also located a pair of prescription eyeglasses at the scene of the crime.

Based on the ransom note, the police questioned three of Bobby Franks's teachers. But suspicion eventually fell on Richard Loeb, in part because Loeb showed an unusual level of interest in the case. Loeb volunteered to assist the police in solving the crime. At one point, a reporter friend of Loeb's asked if Loeb knew Bobby Franks. Loeb responded, "If I were going to murder anybody, I would murder just such a cocky little [kid] as Bobby Franks."

During their investigation the police learned Nathan Leopold was frequently seen bird watching in the area near the crime scene at Wolf Lake. Later, it was also learned that the eyeglasses found near the murder victim were one of only three such pairs sold in Chicago. One pair was sold to Nathan Leopold.

The two suspects were brought in for questioning. Their stories didn't match up and Loeb eventually confessed, followed by Leopold. Thanks to their brilliant attorney, Clarence Darrow, the two youths were

Throughout the trial, the two arrogant young defendants, Nathan Leopold (second from left) and Richard Loeb (third from left), showed little remorse for their crime. Clarence Darrow (right) managed to spare them the death penalty.

Create Your Own Impressionist Painting

Many of the most celebrated works of art owned by the Art Institute of Chicago were created during the late 1800s, when a revolution was taking place among artists, especially in Europe. At this time a new style of painting emerged, which was later called *Impressionism*.

Impressionist paintings are notable in several ways. First, the artists tended to select subjects of everyday life. Instead of depicting gods or important historical figures, Impressionists might paint workers stripping varnish from a floor (*The Floor-Scrapers*, Gustave Caillebotte, 1875). Impressionists also used new techniques, such as blending many different colors to create unique impressions of color and light.

An excellent example of Impressionist painting in the Art Institute of Chicago's collection is Vincent van Gogh's *The Bedroom*. Take a close look at Van Gogh's painting at right. What do you notice about the subject? Do the objects in the room appear to be the right size? Does the furniture look realistic and functional? Does the floor seem to be on an angle? Why do you think the artist chose to distort the perspective?

Try your hand at creating an Impressionist painting.

YOU'LL NEED

Drop cloth or newspapers

Watercolor paper

Pencil

Tempera paint of various colors

Palette (you can use a piece of cardboard with a hole poked out for your thumb)

Brushes

Decide on a real-life subject for your painting, such as your bedroom. The Impressionists also liked to work outdoors, so feel free to select an outdoor scene to paint.

If you are working indoors, make sure to put down a drop cloth or old newspapers, so that you don't make a mess.

Set the watercolor paper down on a flat surface. Using a pencil, lightly sketch the outlines of your subject.

Squeeze small portions of paint from the tubes onto your palette. With your brush, select the color you want to begin with, for example the color of the floor or the wall, and begin painting. Think about the questions above regarding Van Gogh's painting; they will guide you to paint in the Impressionist style.

sentenced to life in prison, rather than the hangman's noose. Before long Loeb was killed by another prison inmate. After serving his sentence Leopold was eventually released from prison and lived the rest of his life in Puerto Rico.

ART RENAISSANCE

In the 1920s the Art Institute of Chicago underwent changes that transformed it into the world-class institution it is today. First, it expanded its building, adding the Goodman Theater space and the McKinlock Memorial Court. More importantly, the museum acquired some of the paintings that it is most famous for today. In 1924 Bertha Palmer's estate donated 52 Impressionist paintings, including works from Claude Monet's series of wheat stack paintings and (Palmer's favorite) Pierre Auguste Renoir's *Acrobats at the Cirque Fernando*, as well as works by Edgar Degas and the American painter Mary Cassatt.

In 1925 the Art Institute acquired perhaps its most famous painting, *A Sunday on La Grande Jatte—1884* by Georges Seurat. *La Grande Jatte* was donated as part of the Helen Birch Bartlett Memorial Collection, along with important works by Vincent van Gogh, Paul Cézanne, and Pablo Picasso.

Vincent van Gogh made several paintings of his bedroom in Arles, France. This version is on display at the Art Institute of Chicago.

VINCENT VAN GOGH, DUTCH, 1853–1890, *THE BEDROOM*, 1889, OIL ON CANVAS, 73.6 X 92.3 CM, HELEN BIRCH BARTLETT MEMORIAL COLLECTION, 1926.417, THE ART INSTITUTE OF CHICAGO. PHOTOGRAPHY © THE ART INSTITUTE OF CHICAGO

9
Gangsters Everywhere

FROM THE TIME Big Bill Thompson took over the mayor's job, Chicago became a "wide open town." In other words, criminals were able to do pretty much whatever they wanted with little opposition from the police. The only thing that stood in the criminals' way was each other. Turf wars were frequent and deadly. But from time to time, thugs managed to stay within their own territories and stay out of each other's business. In the early 1920s Johnny Torrio controlled the largest segment of the city—the South Side and the Loop. He permitted Dion O'Banion to operate on the North Side and Terry Druggan on the West Side—as long as they purchased their

Time Line	
1926	Chicago Blackhawks created; Savoy Big Five (Harlem Globetrotters) introduced; William Wrigley buys Chicago Cubs, renames park Wrigley Field
1927	Richard Wright moves to Chicago; real estate agents promote restrictive covenants; Municipal Airport (later renamed Midway International Airport) opens
1929	Stock Market Crash
1929–mid-1930s	Great Depression
1931	First Bud Billiken Day Parade
1932	Franklin Delano Roosevelt elected president; first pinball machine manufactured in Chicago
1933	Prohibition repealed

Hungry, out-of-work Chicagoans line up for a hot meal at a soup kitchen run by Al Capone during the Depression.
NATIONAL ARCHIVES, ARC ID: 541927

"Chicago seemed to be filled with gangsters—gangsters slaughtering one another, two hundred and fifteen in four years; gangsters being killed by the police, one hundred and sixty in the same length of time; gangsters shooting up saloons for amusement; . . . gangsters strutting in the Loop, holstered pistols scarcely concealed; . . . . gangsters everywhere—except in jail."

—FROM *GEM OF THE PRAIRIE* (1940) BY HERBERT ASBURY

In the early 1920s, Al Capone (1899–1947) was Johnny Torrio's right-hand man, but he would eventually rule just about every aspect of Chicago's organized crime mob.
COURTESY OF KENAN HEISE

supplies from Torrio and didn't stray into neighboring territories. Anyone who stepped out of line found themselves on the deadly end of a tommy gun.

But as with all gangsters, Torrio's time as the top boss was limited. Fortunately for him, he escaped with his life. A practical man who preferred bribes to bump-offs and who spent quiet nights at home with his wife instead of wild nights out with the boys, Torrio planned ahead.

Torrio's troubles started in 1923. He expanded his illegal business dealings to the southwestern suburb of Cicero and then turned the operation of it over to Al "Scarface" Capone. Not the type to be left out, O'Banion demanded a piece of the Cicero action. Torrio let him have a small bit of territory, but O'Banion wasn't satisfied. He decided to double-cross Torrio and Capone by selling them a brewery that he knew was about to be raided by federal

agents. As the deal went down, the police raided the place, and Torrio, Capone, and O'Banion were all three arrested in the setup. Torrio and Capone would later do jail time. O'Banion wouldn't live long enough to join them.

In addition to his illegal businesses, O'Banion also owned a flower store. This might sound like a strange occupation for a hardened criminal, but O'Banion loved flowers and also made a lot of money providing flowers for gangsters' funerals. Mobsters routinely bought expensive flower arrangements for assassinated gangsters—even enemies and even if they were the ones who bumped them off. On November 10, 1924, O'Banion was working overtime at his flower store preparing for another gangster's funeral. He and an assistant were working there when three of Torrio and Capone's men stopped in to pick up a wreath. While one of the three shook hands with O'Banion, the other two "let him have it."

Several days later, O'Banion was the centerpiece for his own gangland funeral. And you can bet that the largest and most expensive flower arrangement at his funeral was sent by Johnny Torrio.

As soon as O'Banion was underground, his partner Hymie Weiss declared war on Torrio and Capone. After several botched attempts, some of his gunmen eventually succeeded in getting to Torrio. They shot Torrio five times on his way home from shopping with his wife. Somehow Torrio survived the attack. At about this time Torrio was due to serve a nine-month jail term for the brewery arrest arranged earlier by O'Banion. Jail turned out to be a safe place to recover from his gunshot wounds

ACTIVITY

Walking Tour: Graceland Cemetery

4001 N. Clark Street, Chicago, Illinois; (773) 525-1105

Call ahead for a schedule of free tours. You can also pay for a guided tour offered by the Chicago History Museum (www.chicagohistory.org) or the Chicago Architecture Foundation (www.architecture.org). When you get to the cemetery, be sure to request a map of the grounds.

Some of Chicago's earliest settlers and prominent citizens are buried at Graceland. Try to find the gravestones for the following individuals: John Kinzie, William B. Ogden (Chicago's first mayor), John Jones, Joseph Medill, Allan Pinkerton, Carter Henry Harrison I and II, Potter and Bertha Palmer, Cyrus Hall McCormick, and Marshall Field.

Graceland not only has some architecturally significant structures (like the Getty Tomb designed by Louis Sullivan), it's also the final resting place of architects Sullivan, Daniel H. Burnham, John Wellborn Root, William Le Baron Jenney, and Ludwig Mies van der Rohe. Also here is a marker for the architectural photographer and preservationist Richard Nickel.

As you walk through the cemetery, see if you can find a baseball-shaped grave stone, a blue grave stone, and a little girl holding an umbrella (Inez Clarke).

Ghost-story fans have said that sometimes Inez mysteriously leaves her perch on the stone, so who knows, she might not be inside her glass box when you get there.

PHOTO BY OWEN HURD

123

and plan his next move. When he got out of jail, Torrio sold Capone his remaining illegal businesses and fled to Italy. Torrio never returned to Chicago, leaving it for Weiss and Capone to fight over.

BRAINS VERSUS BULLETS

Johnny Torrio had always been more of a thinker and a planner than the average gangster. Torrio would rather make a deal than order a "hit." Capone, on the other hand, ruled through terror and force. Maybe that's why Torrio got out of the game. Hymie Weiss wasn't so smart.

Over a period of five years, more than 500 men were killed in Chicago's bloody gang wars. The Weiss gang came pretty close to killing Capone on September 26, 1926. Eleven cars filled with gunmen pulled up alongside a restaurant where Capone was having lunch. Together they shot more than 1,000 bullets into the building, but Capone came out of it without a scratch. The Weiss gang learned if you shoot at Al "Scarface" Capone, you'd better not miss.

A month later, Weiss and one of his henchmen were gunned down in the street outside the office they used above the old flower shop that had been owned by Dion O'Banion. That left George "Bugs" Moran as Capone's only major rival gangster in Chicago. It turned out, though, that Capone didn't need to kill Moran to neutralize him, he just needed to send him a valentine.

A REAL SWEETHEART

Alphonse Capone was now completely in charge of Chicago, even if Bugs Moran was a minor thorn in his side. But Capone didn't want it to look that way. He decided to pretend he had retired from crime, moving to Miami Beach. But of course he still masterminded all the activities of his gang back in Chicago. One of his top henchmen at this time was "Machine Gun" Jack McGurn. A vicious killer, McGurn was always ready to take out anybody that was giving Capone a hard time. Any friend of Capone's was an enemy of Moran's, so it was no surprise when two of Moran's thugs tried to assassinate McGurn.

As McGurn entered a hotel phone booth on Rush Street, he saw Frank and Pete Gusenberg approaching, machine guns in hand. The hit men filled the booth with bullets and quickly made their getaway. But the Gusenberg brothers failed to make sure McGurn was dead—a decision they would live to regret.

McGurn asked for and received Capone's blessing to take out Moran and his shooters for good. On St. Valentine's Day, Thursday, February 14, 1929, McGurn sent a team of assassins over to the S. M. C. Carting Company at 2122 N. Clark Street. The building didn't look like much, but McGurn knew that it was the headquarters for Moran's gang. He also knew that Moran was scheduled to receive a shipment of stolen whiskey that morning. McGurn's gunmen were disguised as policemen.

When the shipment arrived, McGurn's phony policemen stormed the building in a pretend police raid. Back when mobsters bribed police chiefs, judges, and politicians, an arrest for such a small crime was considered no big deal. So Moran's thugs didn't put up a fuss. The fake cops lined the seven members of the Moran gang up against a wall. Moments later, they opened fire with machine guns, shotguns, and revolvers. Both Gusenberg brothers were among the seven killed in the St. Valentine's Day Massacre, but not Bugs Moran. It turns out Moran had overslept and was late for the meeting. As a result he escaped what the next morning's *New York Times* called "the most cold-blooded gang massacre in the history of [Chicago's] underworld."

Police investigators display one of the guns used in the St. Valentine's Day Massacre.
COURTESY OF KENAN HEISE

Nobody was ever convicted of the crime. Capone was in Miami Beach, and McGurn had spent the day at a local hotel, where he made sure he was seen by witnesses who could later provide him with an alibi. One of the victims, Frank Gusenberg, did live for several hours after the shooting, but he refused to identify the killers. Moran may have sidestepped the massacre, but he definitely got the message. From that point on, he restricted his booze-running operations to a very small territory and eventually fell back on smaller criminal activities, such as bank robberies. That way he could steer clear of any more battles with Capone. With all other rivals gone, the only thing Capone had to worry about was the law.

After the St. Valentine's Day Massacre, Capone decided it would be a good idea to lay low for awhile. What better place than in jail? Capone actually arranged to have himself arrested. He tipped off a couple of Philadelphia cops that he would be in the neighborhood and carrying a gun. The detectives met Capone at the agreed-upon location. Capone promptly handed over the gun and a $20,000 payoff for the favor of arresting him. Capone was sentenced to one year in jail, just enough time to let things settle down.

THE UNTOUCHABLES

While Capone had been taking over the rackets in Chicago, a young crime fighter was beginning to make a name for himself. Eliot Ness, an inexperienced employee of the Department of Justice's Prohibition Bureau, joined a team of federal and local law enforcement officers in the effort to bring down Capone's liquor operations. Ness led a series of daring raids on Capone's underground breweries, arresting Capone's henchmen and confiscating distillery equipment. The *Chicago Tribune* gave Ness and his men the nickname "Untouchables," because they refused to accept bribes from the gangs.

Some people have argued that Ness played a relatively small role in bringing down Capone. Despite all the raids and arrests, Ness never compiled enough evidence to successfully convict Capone of any crimes. The raids were probably little more than a nuisance to Capone. Members of Capone's gang rarely put up much of a struggle in these raids and readily surrendered to arrest. Because Capone had paid off so many judges, his men knew they would be back on the streets in no time.

The U.S. Attorney in charge of the Capone investigation, George E. Q. Johnson, encouraged Ness to keep the pressure on Capone. But he was also conducting a separate investigation into Capone's finances,

Publicity Wars

ELIOT NESS WAS A publicity hound. He always made sure to coordinate his raids with newspaper reporters and photographers so that the next day's paper would include a picture of him catching the criminals or smashing wooden beer kegs with a sledgehammer. But not everyone was in favor of the Prohibition Act, so sometimes this publicity backfired.

Capone also used the media to his advantage. One of the most effective ways he tried to get public opinion on his side was to feed the poor and hungry during the Depression. On December 5, 1930, the *Chicago Tribune* threw Capone a bone with the following headline: "120,000 Meals Are Served by Capone Free Soup Kitchens."

But Capone ultimately lost the publicity war when Frank J. Loesch, the head of the Chicago Crime Commission, came up with the Public Enemies List. When Capone was declared Public Enemy Number One, he lost much of his popular support.

headed by Internal Revenue Service (IRS) agent Frank Wilson. Wilson gathered information using undercover agents as well as criminal associates of Capone, such as dog racetrack owner and gambling insider Eddie O'Hare.

On June 5, 1931, the government had assembled enough evidence to indict Capone with 22 counts of failing to pay his taxes, a crime known as tax evasion. The prosecution would attempt to prove that Capone had failed to pay $215,000 in taxes on over $1 million in income earned between 1925 and 1929. A week later, the government brought more charges against Capone based on Ness's investigations into Capone's bootlegging, but Capone never went to trial for them.

Instead, Capone was found guilty on five counts of tax evasion and sentenced to 11 years in jail with fines of over $80,000. The money was a drop in the bucket to Capone, but the length of jail time was a shock. It was the stiffest sentence ever handed down for tax evasion.

Capone's reign of terror in Chicago was over. His health, spirit, and sanity all deteriorated during his prison term. When he was released from jail in 1939, Capone was a shadow of the man he once was. He spent the rest of his life in quiet seclusion,

AND CHICAGO IS ABOUT TO LOSE ITS BAD REPUTATION

This cartoon appeared on the front page of the *Chicago Tribune*, June 15, 1931.
CHICAGO TRIBUNE

The Nebraska "Ness"

BELIEVE IT OR NOT, Al Capone's older brother, Vincenzo Capone, was actually a law enforcement official. Changing his name to Richard Hart, he led Prohibition-era raids on Nebraska breweries in the same manner as Eliot Ness did in Chicago. Known for being well armed during these raids, Capone's brother came to be known as "Two-Gun" Hart. Once, while visiting his notorious brother in Chicago, Hart was asked if he would ever arrest members of Capone's gang. Not as long as they stayed out of Nebraska, he replied.

cared for by his family. His business interests were sharply reduced by now, as all decisions were now made by his brothers. Capone died on January 25, 1947, and was buried at Mt. Olivet Cemetery. Later, his body was exhumed by family and reburied at Mt. Carmel.

THE PEOPLE'S CROOKS

While organized crime boss Capone was imprisoned at Alcatraz Island, the public's fascination with celebrity criminals turned to a different breed of hoodlum, the lone gunman—or gunwoman—who robbed banks and escaped through a hail of bullets: "Ma" Barker and her son "Doc" Barker, Bonnie Parker and Clyde Barrow, "Pretty Boy" Floyd, "Baby Face" Nelson, and

"Machine Gun" Kelly. The colorful names and daring exploits grabbed headlines of the nation's newspapers and captured the imaginations of the American public. During the Depression, many of the downtrodden blamed the government and banks for their hardships. So it was not unusual for the public to consider these robbers heroes, almost like Robin Hoods. They sure knew how to steal from the rich—but somehow never got around to giving to the poor.

Perhaps the most daring gunslinging bankrobber of the times was John Dillinger. During a crime spree across the Midwest, Dillinger pulled off 10 bank robberies and three jailbreaks. In this time he stole about $300,000 and shot 10 people, earning him a spot on the FBI's Most Wanted List. Investigators got a tip that Dillinger would

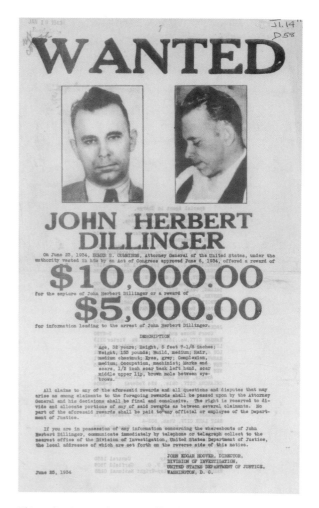

This police Wanted poster offered rewards for information about John Dillinger.
NATIONAL ARCHIVES, ARC ID: 306713

be going to Chicago's Biograph movie theater on July 22, 1934, escorted by a woman wearing an orange skirt. Agents witnessed Dillinger entering the theater to see a Clark Gable gangster film, called *Manhattan Melodrama*.

After the movie was over, Dillinger walked out of the theater and into a trap. Dillinger ran toward an alley and went for his gun. Before he could reach either one, officers gunned him down, shooting him in the back.

JAZZ AGE

The 1920s in Chicago may have been dominated by gangsters, but this period was also the height of the Jazz Age. In 1922 a young trumpet player named Louis Armstrong moved to Chicago to make a name for himself in Chicago's thriving jazz scene. Armstrong joined Joe "King" Oliver's Creole Jazz Band and quickly became the most celebrated jazz trumpeter in the city. Armstrong eventually moved to New York, where he became a worldwide star, but Chicago's jazz scene continued to grow and attract more fans.

Throughout the 1920s, most of Chicago's jazz bands were made up of African American musicians performing mostly for audiences on the South Side. Clubs like the Royal Gardens Café, Dreamland Café, and Sunset Café were popular places to see jazz entertainers, such as Earl Hines (piano), Johnny Dodds (clarinet), and Warren "Baby" Dodds (drummer). Some of these audiences included young white jazz fans who later joined the next generation of Chicago's jazz musicians. Jimmy McPartland, Bud Freeman, Benny Goodman, and Gene Krupa were some of the more famous white jazz musicians who learned how to play in Chicago. More jazz clubs and music halls opened throughout the city, including the famous Green Mill in the North Side Uptown neighborhood.

With all these musicians in town, Chicago also became a major center for jazz recording studios. Unfortunately, by the early 1930s many of the artists who helped develop the "Chicago sound" had moved to New York.

Close, But No Cigar

THE CHICAGO CUBS made it back to the World Series again in 1932, but Babe Ruth once again kept them from winning. In 1918 Ruth beat them from the pitcher's mound as a member of the Boston Red Sox. In 1932, he did it from the batter's box where he slugged a famously long home run off the center field scoreboard. Some say the Babe "called the shot" by pointing his bat toward center field just before hitting the towering homer.

10

The City Turns a Century

WITH ITS GANGSTERS and corruption, Chicago was getting a reputation in the world that the city's law-abiding citizens wanted to change. As early as 1924 the city's civic leaders were looking for ways to show that Chicago was a world-class city, still capable of the magnificence it had displayed during the 1893 World's Columbian Exposition. What Chicago needed was another world's fair. What better time to throw it than on the occasion of the city's 100th birthday? Chicago received Congressional approval to host the 1933 World's Fair, which was dubbed the Century of Progress.

Time Line

1933 Chicago celebrates 100th birthday by hosting the World's Fair

1940 Chicago appoints nation's first African American police captain

1941 Orchard Field (later renamed O'Hare International Airport) opens

1943 Chicago's first subway opens

1947 Michigan Avenue north of the Chicago River dubbed the "Magnificent Mile"

1948 Meigs Field opens

A drawing of the Century of Progress fairgrounds in 1933.

COURTESY OF KENAN HEISE

Chicago had, of course, changed quite a bit in 100 years. Its first citizens, Jean Baptiste Point Du Sable, John Kinzie, Mark Beaubien, and Gurdon Hubbard would scarcely recognize the place. From 350 inhabitants in 1833, the city's population had now skyrocketed to nearly 3.5 million.

In 1833 Chicago covered just six square miles of land in the area immediately surrounding where the Chicago River meets Lake Michigan. Since then Chicago had stretched north, south, and west, sweeping up small towns dotting the city's outskirts.

Architectural Cemetery

A LOT OF WONDERFUL buildings went up during this era, but a lot of architectural treasures also came down. George Pullman's Prairie Avenue mansion, at the northeast corner of 18th and Prairie, was demolished in 1922. When George Pullman's widow died, her will specified that the mansion be torn down, because she couldn't stand the idea of anyone else living in her home. Burnham's Illinois Trust & Savings Bank (erected in 1897) was demolished in 1924. The second Palmer House, built just after the Great Chicago Fire, also bit the dust in 1925. Holabird & Roche's Tacoma Building (1889) was demolished in 1929, followed by the Marshall Field Wholesale Store (1885) in 1930. William Le Baron Jenney's Home Insurance Building (1885), the world's first modern skyscraper, was razed in 1931.

Chicago's skyline as it appeared shortly before the 1933 fair.
LIBRARY OF CONGRESS, LC-USZC2-5810

Chicago had even expanded eastward, filling the lake in with debris from the Chicago Fire, as well as from the constant building, destruction, and rebuilding of the ever-changing city. By 1933 Chicago had swelled to about 200 square miles (currently 228.5 square miles).

The 100-year-old Chicago had grown outward and upward. By 1933 Chicago was the home of massive structures, including many of the buildings that Chicago is famous for to this day. Commercial buildings that went up at this time include the Drake Hotel (built in 1920), Wrigley Building (1924), Tribune Tower (1925), Palmolive Building (1929), Carbide & Carbon Building (1929), Medinah Athletic Club (1929), Merchandise Mart (1930), Chicago Board of Trade (1930), and the Skyline Century of Progress (1930).

A number of cultural buildings were also erected during this building boom. Soldier Field (1926), the John G. Shedd Aquarium (1929), and the Adler Planetarium (1930) joined the Field Museum at the southern end of Grant Park to create Chicago's "Museum Campus." Another important addition to Chicago's cultural scene was the Civic Opera Building (1929), which takes up the entire block of North Wacker Drive from Madison to Washington. Soaring 555 feet into the air, the Civic casts a modern

Bungalows

SKYSCRAPERS GET ALL the headlines, but what would Chicago architecture be without its bungalows, those one-and-a-half story brick homes lining so many of the city's neighborhood streets? These buildings aren't exactly what you'd call architectural masterpieces, but they give a unique character to Chicago's housing. The thousands of bungalows built in the 1920s and 1930s provided affordable housing for Chicago's growing middle class.

Typical Chicago brick bungalows.
PHOTO BY OWEN HURD

shadow on Wolf Point, the former site of Mark Beaubien's Sauganash Hotel. In 1933 the Museum of Science and Industry moved into its current home, the only permanent building constructed for the 1893 World's Columbian Exposition.

Chicago was also expanding its roads and bridges to meet the demands of the city's growing population and industry. The Michigan Avenue Bridge (1920) brought Michigan Avenue north across the Chicago River. If it weren't for the Michigan Avenue Bridge, two of Chicago's architectural treasures—the Wrigley Building and the Tribune Tower—probably wouldn't have been built north of the Chicago River. Previously known as Pine Street, the northern section of Michigan Avenue would later rival the State Street shopping district.

Two other massive road-building projects took place at about this time. Wacker Drive became Chicago's first double-decker street in 1926, and Lake Shore Drive opened in 1933. Chicago's growth spurt didn't ignore newer forms of transportation. As air travel became more popular, Chicago opened its first major airport in 1927. Originally called Chicago Municipal Airport, it was later renamed Midway Airport to commemorate the World War II Battle of Midway.

A FAIR TO REMEMBER

The idea to host another world's fair was hatched during the Roaring Twenties, when Chicago, like most of the country, was enjoying great prosperity, growth, and progress. Many industries at this time were benefiting from new ways to manufacture, sell, and transport goods. The Century of Progress World's Fair would put these advancements on display.

Nobody had any reason to believe that the boom times would go away any time soon. So, on October 28, 1929, the corporation set up to organize the fair offered $10 million in bonds for public sale to fund the fair. On the very next day the stock market crashed, sending the economy into a downward spiral. Forty years after the Columbian Exposition, Chicago once again found itself trying to finance a world's fair in the middle of an economic depression. But Chicago and its citizens were too proud and too determined to fail, especially with the whole world watching. Ed Kelly, Chicago's mayor from 1933 to 1947, would later boast that "only Chicago would have had the courage to plan and realize such a fair when the whole world was suffering from a depression."

With people struggling to afford essentials like food and shelter, they obviously didn't have money to spend on bonds to fund the fair. So it was up to Chicago's civic leaders. Rufus C. Dawes persuaded a number of wealthy Chicagoans to pledge up to $9 million—enough to keep the effort moving forward. Eventually, average citizens were encouraged by the progress of the fair to pitch in too. Chicagoans bought their tickets to the fair in advance, which provided the fair project much-needed construction funds.

Bad Omen

IN CHICAGO'S HISTORY, two of its mayors have been assassinated, both in years that the city was hosting a world's fair. Carter Harrison was murdered at the close of the 1893 World's Columbian Exposition in 1893. Chicago mayor Anton Cermak was killed just two months before opening day of the 1933 Century of Progress fair. Cermak was traveling in Florida with Franklin Delano Roosevelt. An assassin's bullet intended for FDR struck Cermak instead. To replace Cermak, the City Council elected Edward J. Kelly, who became the mayor of Chicago during the Century of Progress fair.

"Breath-taking thrills, strange attractions, freaks, dancers, . . . Lilliputians in Midget Village—in a city of a million lights—performing in a tempo of a new day. Here one may test all the new devices, including roller coasters, flying turns, shooting rapids, caterpillar glides, and so on without end."—FROM *CHICAGO AND ITS TWO WORLD'S FAIRS* (1933)

KID STUFF

In addition to the usual scientific exhibits, this fair also had its share of fun and games. There were amusement park rides, like roller coasters and the Sky Ride. Carrying passengers across a lagoon 200 feet in the air, the Sky Ride was the 1933 fair's answer to the Ferris wheel 40 years earlier. The Enchanted Island and Magic Mountain were favorite attractions for kids. Though inappropriate by today's standards, the Midget Village and other "freak shows" were also popular with children as well as adults.

The fair helped Chicagoans, Americans, and foreign visitors forget some of the problems that they faced in the Great Depression. It was such a great success that the organizers decided to keep the buildings up and reopen the exhibits in the following year. In all, about 10 million visitors came to the Century of Progress World's Fair in Chicago—twice as many as the World's Columbian Exposition 40 years earlier.

The Enchanted Island attraction at the Century of Progress World's Fair.
COURTESY OF KENAN HEISE

This helped the local economy immensely. In the *Chicago Tribune*, the owner of one retail store said that 1933 sales were up 54 percent from the previous year. It's no wonder that the city decided not to close up the fair after one season.

At the Chicago Day celebration, October 9, 1933, Chicago Mayor Ed Kelly offered a second reason to reopen the fair in 1934. The extra year would give locals who had "been so busy being host" to partake in the fair themselves. Unfortunately many Chicagoans simply could not afford the luxury of the fair's amusements or to shop at fancy State Street stores. Chicago was

Two Chips off the Burnham Block

DANIEL H. BURNHAM, the head architect of Chicago's previous world's fair, the World's Columbian Exposition of 1893, had died in 1912. Fortunately, two of his sons were on hand in 1933 to help plan and build the Century of Progress fair. Daniel H. Burnham Jr. was appointed to the architectural committee. His brother Hubert Burnham designed several of the fair's buildings.

Policemen charge unarmed picketers protesting against Republic Steel. The Memorial Day Massacre was the most deadly labor event since the Haymarket bombing and riot.
NATIONAL ARCHIVES, ARC ID: 306197

especially hard hit by the Depression. Half of the workforce was out of work. Banks were failing. Many people were homeless or living in squalid conditions.

The Chicagoans who did have jobs often found that they weren't making enough to get by. Public school teachers went unpaid for months at a time. Companies were laying off workers or reducing their hours and pay. Many workers joined and supported unions to fight for their rights. Workers' unions helped organize strikes and other forms of protest.

One demonstration, on May 30, 1937, proved deadly. Striking workers had intended to picket at Republic Steel.

When police were called in to disperse the protesters, skirmishes broke out. Swinging clubs and shooting pistols, the police killed 10 and wounded many more. This tragic event, which came to be known as the Memorial Day Massacre, was a new low point in Chicago labor history.

Some relief came in the form of government aid and jobs. Under the leadership of Franklin Delano Roosevelt, the federal government created a number of programs designed to help people get through the tough times and to kick start the economy. These programs came to be known as the New Deal. The Social Security Administration was set up to help the unemployed and the aged. The U.S. government also provided money to local governments to create jobs through public works projects. In Chicago, federal money helped finance building projects, such as the State Street subway, a new water intake crib in Lake Michigan, and completion of Midway Airport and Lake Shore Drive.

Skilled and unskilled laborers weren't the only ones helped out by Franklin Roosevelt's New Deal policies. The Works Progress Administration (WPA) employed many Chicago artists, performers, and writers, who of course also suffered during the Depression. Many of the murals painted in

Monsters of the Midway

THE CHICAGO BEARS used to play their home games at Wrigley Field, and got their name from the fact that the football players were bigger than the baseball players who used Wrigley Field in the summer. Under the leadership of owner-coach George Halas, the Bears won NFL championships in 1932 and 1940. The Bears continued to dominate the NFL, winning three more championships over the next six seasons.

The Chicago Bears celebrate their 73-0 victory over the Washington Redskins in the 1940 national title game.
COURTESY OF KENAN HEISE

137

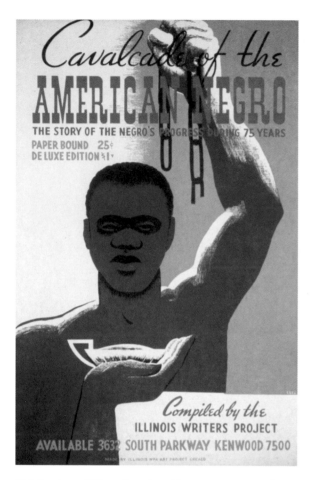

This book on African American history was one product of the Illinois Writers Project.

The WPA also produced posters, like this one promoting free art classes at Hull House.

the city's public schools, libraries, and post offices were created at this time. Writers such as Nelson Algren, Saul Bellow, Studs Terkel, and Richard Wright participated in the Federal Writers Project. WPA funds were also used to support theater companies, such as the Chicago Negro Company.

In addition to government assistance, private relief agencies also stepped in. Jane Addams died in 1935, but Hull House continued to help needy Chicagoans throughout the Depression and up to this day.

Relief efforts helped countless Chicagoans make it through the Depression. Unfortunately, the only thing that managed to bring the U.S. economy completely out of the Depression was another world war. As it was with World War I, increased demand for war materials meant more production and more jobs. Almost overnight, unemployment in Chicago went from 50 percent to 1 percent.

Of course, World War II also meant worldwide suffering and destruction. Approximately 62 million people were killed during World War II, and entire cities were destroyed in bombings. Although enemy war planes never made it to the U.S. mainland, much less to Chicago, tens of thousands of Chicagoans were sent to fight overseas. Thousands never returned.

New Deal in Chicago

THE DEMOCRATIC PARTY held its national convention at the Chicago Stadium from June 27 to July 2, 1932. This is where Franklin D. Roosevelt unveiled his plans for the New Deal, proclaiming, "I pledge you, I pledge myself, a new deal for the American people."

TO WAR

In 1933, the same year Chicago was celebrating its 100th birthday, Adolf Hitler came to power in Germany. Six years later World War II would begin when Germany invaded Poland and then France. The United States did not immediately join the war. Like many other Americans, Chicagoans were divided on whether or not to take part in the European war. The decision was made for them on December 7, 1941, when Germany's ally, Japan, bombed the U.S. naval base at Pearl Harbor, Hawaii.

Chicago sent many of its sons and daughters overseas to fight in World War II, but the people who stayed behind faced their share of hardships as well. Many Chicagoans suffered from loneliness and anxiety being separated from loved ones sent overseas. They also faced shortages of food, clothing, and fuel.

On the home front, people were expected to be patriotic and brave, to keep spirits high. They were also expected to hate the enemy, buy war bonds to raise money for the war effort, and work in factories to make the supplies needed to fight the enemy. Chicagoans were asked to plant "victory gardens" in their backyards to help ease food shortages, and to participate in scrap drives to collect raw materials to be made into weapons and other items needed by the military.

There was no shortage of fear. Throughout the war Chicagoans worried that their city could be bombed by Japanese or German planes. Many kids kept a lookout for these attack planes and played with war-themed toys such as military figurines, toy tanks, and planes. Fortunately, blackouts, gas masks, air raid sirens, and air raid wardens turned out to be an unnecessary precaution during World War II.

This poster reminded Chicagoans that attractions like Buckingham Fountain in Grant Park were always free. Programs like these also helped by employing artists to design the posters.

LIBRARY OF CONGRESS, LC-USZC4-5158

WOMEN RISE TO THE CHALLENGE

One of the great stories about World War II was the way women pitched in, both at home and on the battle lines. Some served in the U.S. armed forces. And with many of the city's workers fighting overseas, women also did their part by working in the factories, producing aircraft, radios, and ammunition. Others worked as typists, stenographers, bookkeepers, and speechwriters. During the war about 300,000 Chicago women were working outside the home, more than double the number before the war.

At these times, social service agencies had a shortage of employees, so many women also volunteered to help out with local agencies providing childcare and health care services. They also volunteered to bake cookies and cakes for military recreation centers set up to entertain soldiers on leave.

RACIAL TENSIONS

World War II made life especially difficult for German, Italian, and Japanese immigrants living in Chicago because people feared that people from these countries might sympathize with the United States' enemies. Members of these ethnic groups—and sometimes others—were harassed and

As this poster shows, Chicagoans of all ages were expected to do their part to help the war effort. Scrap drives to collect paper, rubber, and metal were an everyday occurrence.
CHICAGO HISTORY MUSEUM, ICHI-25511

Children at a predominantly African American public school in Chicago raised $263,148.83 for the war effort.

NATIONAL ARCHIVES, ARC ID: 535815

National Champs

DEPAUL UNIVERSITY'S men's college basketball team won the national championship in 1945. The Blue Demons were led by their seven-foot-tall center, George Mikan, and coached by Ray Meyer. Mikan was the team's lead scorer, but he had an even bigger impact on defense. Camped out beneath the opposing team's basket, Mikan would swat away shot after shot. The NCAA later passed a new rule to outlaw "goal tending."

DePaul coach Ray Meyer holds the championship trophy. Center George Mikan (wearing eyeglasses) is standing behind Meyer.

DEPAUL UNIVERSITY

on rare occasions the victims of violence. For these reasons Germans, Italians, and Japanese were eager to show their allegiance to the United States. Their young men and women served loyally and bravely in the armed forces. They also volunteered on the home front.

Before World War II, the Japanese population in Chicago was very small: about 350 Japanese lived throughout the city. Immediately following the bombing of Pearl Harbor there were a few incidents of violence, including the smashing of windows at a Japanese gift shop. For the most part, however, Japanese living in Chicago were actually treated more fairly than in other areas of the country. Out west, Japanese were imprisoned in internment camps, and their property was taken from them. In Chicago they were permitted to live freely and work. In fact, about 20,000 Japanese Americans were eventually released from internment camps in the west and transported to Chicago during the war. In Chicago, Japanese Americans found work in the factories making aircraft, electronics, and other materials needed for the war effort.

Chinese and Filipinos living in Chicago were eager to make sure they weren't mistaken for Japanese. Some went so far as to wear badges identifying themselves as loyal

A Street in Bronzeville

IN THE 1940S BRONZEVILLE—the area bordered by 22nd Street, 51st Street, Cottage Grove Road, and the Rock Island rail line—was the focal point of culture and creativity in Chicago's African American community. Bronzeville was home to rich and poor African Americans alike.

Bronzeville was also the home of a young girl named Gwendolyn Brooks who wrote poems about what she saw and heard growing up on the South Side of Chicago. A collection of her poems called *A Street in Bronzeville* was published in 1945. Brooks won the Pulitzer Prize in 1950 and went on to become poet laureate of Illinois.

A SONG IN THE FRONT YARD
I've stayed in the front yard all my life.
I want a peek at the back
Where it's rough and untended and hungry weed grows.
A girl gets sick of a rose.

I want to go in the back yard now
And maybe down the alley,
To where the charity children play.
I want a good time today.

They do some wonderful things.
They have some wonderful fun.
My mother sneers, but I say it's fine
How they don't have to go in at quarter to nine.

—from *A Street in Bronzeville* (1945) by Gwendolyn Brooks, reprinted by consent of Brooks Permissions

Americans. World War II also made life in America uneasy for German immigrants and their native-born descendants. Some changed their last names or the names of their businesses to make them sound less German.

Demand for machinery, supplies, weapons, and ammunition created a huge demand for labor. As was the case with World War I, African Americans benefited from the need for more workers. Unfortunately, they were still treated like second-class citizens, despite their patriotism and despite their commitment to the cause of freedom. Some African Americans organized marches to protest the situation. Others who were denied jobs on the home front simply decided to sign up in the armed forces. Uncle Sam was glad to put them to work.

MANHATTAN IN CHICAGO

In April 1945 Adolf Hitler committed suicide, and the Germans surrendered. But the war with Japan continued. Only a handful of people knew it at the time, but the world's most powerful weapon was being developed in the city of Chicago. Code-named the Manhattan Project, the secret program would ultimately play a key role in ending the Second World War. In 1942 scientists working at the University of Chicago performed experiments that led to the creation of the first atomic bombs. By creating the world's first atomic reactor, these scientists, including Arthur H. Compton and Italian Enrico Fermi, made possible the bombs dropped on Hiroshima and Nagasaki in August 1945.

The Allied forces were on the verge of winning the war even without the bomb, but the decision to use the bomb was made in the hopes of shortening the war and reducing the number of Allied soldiers killed. The bomb helped the Allies win the war, but victory came with an unimaginable cost—not only for those killed, but for all who now lived in a world where nuclear war was possible.

ACTIVITY

Write a Poem About Your Street

Gwendolyn Brooks obviously had a special talent, but anyone can write poetry. Take a shot at writing your own poem about the street you live on.

Start by taking notes. Be as descriptive as you can. A good way to think of ideas is to make a list of the things you can see, hear, smell, taste, and touch. Try to notice the colors, textures, and shapes of things in your neighborhood. Next write down those things that say something about what it's like to live in your neighborhood. Try to recall specific people, places, and events.

When you've filled a page or so, take some time to review your notes. Pick out specific phrases that you like. String them together. Then, if you choose, try to think of words that rhyme with the last words in those phrases and play around with different ideas. Most of all don't worry about trying to make your poem a piece of art. Just relax and have fun and you should be able to produce something that you can be proud of.

11
Economic Growth, Political Upheaval

Time Line

1945 World War II ends; Cubs lose World Series

1955 Emmett Till murdered; Richard J. Daley elected to first mayoral term

1957 Old Town School of Folk Music opens

1958 Inland Steel Building built; fire at Our Lady of the Angels school kills 92 students and three nuns

1959 White Sox win American League pennant, lose World Series

1963 Loyola University wins NCAA tournament; Bears win NFL championship

1966 Dr. Martin Luther King Jr. moves to Chicago, leads housing protests

1968 Riots break out on Chicago's West Side after Martin Luther King is assassinated in April; Democratic Convention in Chicago erupts in violence

1969 Black Panther Fred Hampton killed in police raid; John Hancock Center built

1972 Chicago Stock Exchange demolished

1974 Sears Tower built

1976 Richard J. Daley dies

THE FRONT-PAGE HEADLINE of the *Chicago Sun* newspaper on August 14, 1945, said it all: "It's Over! It's Peace! It's Victory!" Finally, the Allied forces (including Poland, France, the United Kingdom, and later, the Soviet Union and the United States) had prevailed over the Axis powers (Nazi Germany, Japan, and Italy). Chicagoans could join in celebrating the end of the fighting, the end of the atrocities, and the end of home-front hardships. Victory in Europe followed by victory in Japan brought joy and hope. But the end of the war also brought a whole new set of fears and doubts. After all, things had been pretty bad before the war had started.

Chicagoans party in the streets of the Loop to celebrate the end of the World War II.

CHICAGO HISTORY MUSEUM, ICHI-35018, PHOTO BY GORDON COSTER

Would things go back to the way they were before the war? Would the Depression return?

As a result of the Great Depression and World War II, Chicago's growth and development had come to a standstill. No new skyscrapers had been built. Many companies went out of business during the Depression or scaled back production, laying off workers. The companies that survived the Depression focused most of their energies on making products needed to win the war. That would all change in the coming postwar years, as Chicago got back to work.

Many feared that after the war Chicago and the rest of the country would be hit by another depression. It's true that the military no longer needed so many airplanes, tanks, jeeps, weapons, and ammunition. Many Chicagoans who worked at these factories did lose their jobs when the war ended. However, many of these factories were able to go back to building the things they used to manufacture before the war. For example, the Pullman Company, which had switched to shipbuilding during the war, could now return to making train cars. During the war, the Chicago Bridge and Iron Company built hundreds of amphibious crafts used for beach invasions. After the war, the company returned to making iron supports for bridges and other large structures.

It turned out that the feared postwar depression never happened. One reason was savings. Not only had the government set aside a large amount of money for postwar public works projects, most families had a nest egg to fall back on too. Many Chicagoans had worked overtime during the war, making higher than usual wages. And because they were encouraged to buy war bonds, many people found themselves with more savings than ever before.

Chicagoans had money to buy homes, which fed a housing boom, especially out in the rapidly growing Chicago suburbs. They also had money to fill those homes with consumer goods like radios, televisions, refrigerators, washers, and dryers. Thousands of companies that had manufactured goods for the war now turned to producing goods that consumers wanted and could afford. Other Chicagoans decided to invest in education, paying for college with savings and government loans. Others still used their money to start new businesses or to invest in real estate.

In a way, the end of the war finally made it possible for Chicago and the world to take advantage of the technology and progress celebrated 12 years earlier at the Century of Progress World's Fair. Dreams that were put on hold during the Depression and the war

The Cubs' Curse

IT WOULD TAKE A WHILE before life returned to normal in Chicago. It may have helped that the Chicago Cubs were in the World Series for the first time in decades. After five games, the Cubs trailed the Detroit Tigers 3 games to 2. Needing to win the final two games, the Cubs won an extra-inning thriller in game 6. But their luck ran out the next day when the Tigers won 9–3. The Cubs haven't been back to the World Series since.

To this day, some Cubs fans still blame the Curse of the Billy Goat for the North Siders' losing ways. Chicago restaurant owner William "Billy Goat" Sianis tried to bring his goat with him to game four—he even bought his mascot a ticket to the game. Wrigley Field guards turned Sianis and his goat away. Angry with the Cubs for foiling his publicity stunt, Sianis hexed the Cubs, swearing that they'd never win another World Series. So far, the curse is still intact.

Back to School

AFTER WORLD WAR II Chicago experienced its second period of architectural innovation, called the Second Chicago School of Architecture. One of the most influential pioneers during this time was Ludwig Mies van der Rohe (1886–1969), a German-born architect who moved to Chicago in 1937 to head up the architecture department at what is now called the Illinois Institute of Technology. As the father of the Second Chicago School of Architecture, Mies designed many notable structures in Chicago, including the Chicago Federal Center, Commonwealth Plaza Apartments at 330–340 W. Diversey, and especially the apartment towers at 860–880 N. Lake Shore Drive. Mies' influence is also clearly seen in most of the modernist structures built in Chicago after World War II.

The John Hancock Center is the third-tallest building in Chicago, after the Sears Tower and Aon Center.
PHOTO BY OWEN HURD

could now be realized. To win the war, manufacturers in the United States had discovered ways to make products faster and better. They developed new ideas and improved old ones, like business management, quality control, and efficiency.

With the postwar economy booming, Chicago got back to building. The first major public works projects were the many bridges, parks, schools, and highways that were built in the years after the war. In 1958 the Inland Steel Building at 30 West Monroe was completed. Designed by Skidmore, Owings & Merrill (SOM), it was among the first skyscrapers built in Chicago in over 20 years.

The architects at SOM also designed the two modern architectural giants that most tourists flock to in Chicago: the John Hancock Center (1969) and the Sears Tower (1974). Crisscrossed with X-shaped supports that run from top to bottom of the building's 100 stories, the Hancock is the more architecturally stunning.

Once the world's tallest building at 1,450 feet, the Sears Tower wins for engineering genius. The building and surrounding plazas take up three acres of city ground, while the building's 110 stories contain more than 101 acres of usable square footage. About 25,000 people enter the building each day,

Architectural Walking Tour: Modern Skyscrapers

The skyscrapers that were built in Chicago after World War II appear to have a totally different style than those built in the late 1800s and early 1900s. However, these buildings are using some of the basic ideas that were established by architects who designed Chicago's historic skyscrapers. Following Louis Sullivan's principle that form should follow function, these buildings were designed with specific uses in mind, usually business and governmental functions.

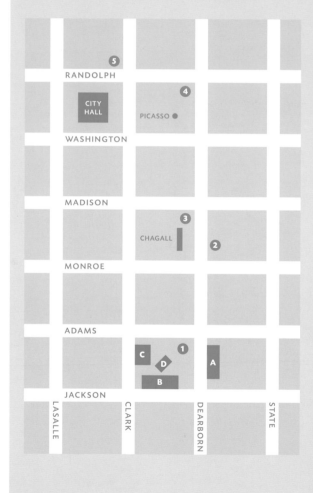

As you walk the route of the tour below, consider the following questions:

What are the building's physical characteristics? How many stories does it have? What building materials were used?

How would you describe the style? Classical or modern? Sleek or bulky? Ornate or plain? Do doorways and windows employ curved arches or are they square/rectangular? Is the design symmetrical or imbalanced?

The tour should take approximately two hours. Start at the southwest corner of Dearborn and Adams.

Chicago Federal Center (1)
Architects: Ludwig Mies van der Rohe; Schmidt, Garden & Erikson; C. F. Murphy Associates; A. Epstein & Sons

Everett McKinley Dirksen Building (1959–64) (A)
219 S. Dearborn Street

John C. Kluczynski Federal Building (1966–74) (B)
230 S. Dearborn Street

U.S. Post Office (1966–74) (C)
219 S. Clark

These buildings may look fairly plain to the untrained eye, but that's the point. Mies van der Rohe was working under the theory that less is more. By stripping away the unnecessary elements he attempted to create a simple, plain beauty. Do you think he succeeded?

The two taller buildings feature some of the hallmarks of modern skyscrapers: exposed columns, recessed main floors, as well as uniformity and repetition of geometric patterns.

In several ways the architects also attempted to unify the three buildings—to make them seem like they belong together. Obviously the three buildings are all made of the same materials. They are also connected by a geometrical logic. Look down at one of the paving stones on the plaza. Follow the lines between the pavers toward any of the three buildings. Notice how each one lines up with the vertical supports on each building.

Before you move on to the next stop in the tour, look at the sculpture (D) in the plaza, and guess what the title might be. Did you guess *Flamingo*?

Walk one block north to the northeast corner of Dearborn and Monroe.

Inland Steel (2)
30 W. Monroe
Architects: Skidmore, Owings & Merrill (1958)

When you first look at this building, you might ask yourself: What's so great about that? It certainly isn't the tallest, and it probably doesn't look like the most innovative. But the building did break important ground in several ways. A clue to this building's uniqueness is visible at the back of the building. Notice the thin windowless tower connected on the east side of the Inland Steel Building. What do you think it's for? By placing the bathrooms, stairways, and elevators in this tower, the architects were able to maximize the usable floor space of the offices in the main building. Uncluttered with walls and stair wells, each floor has an open feeling, inviting plenty of natural light.

The next stop on the tour is across Dearborn Street.

Chase Tower (3)
Architect: Perkins & Will; C. F. Murphy Associates (1969)

One thing you've probably noticed about modern buildings is the presence of public art, which is now required by the city's development guidelines. Marc Chagall's mural *The Four Seasons* is one of the most famous examples. The area to the south of Chase Tower also features an inviting plaza. A minimum amount of public space is also required for commercial and government buildings.

Stand at the base of the southeast corner of the building. With your back to the main support look straight up. Notice the dramatic curve in the structure's main supports. The building's design maximizes the main floor space for banking customers. The thinner top floors help to preserve the amount of access to natural light for surrounding streets and buildings.

Walk one block north to the northwest corner of Dearborn and Washington.

Richard J. Daley Center (4)
Block bounded by W. Washington, W. Randolph, N. Dearborn, and N. Clark Streets

Architects: C. F. Murphy Associates; Loebl, Schlossman & Bennett; Skidmore, Owings & Merrill (1965)

Similar in style to the Federal Center buildings, the Daley Center is supported by columns made of Cor-ten steel, which were designed to rust. Notice the drains at the bases of these columns. These permit rusty rainwater to drain off the columns without staining the concrete plaza. The Picasso sculpture in the Daley Center Plaza is made of the same steel. There's a long-running debate about this modern sculpture. Do you think it looks more like a dog or a woman? Walk around the sculpture observing it from various perspectives. You may even see the profile of Richard J. Daley.

Walk one block north and one block west to the northwest corner of Randolph and Clark.

James R. Thompson Center (5)
100 W. Randolph

Architects: Murphy/Helmut Jahn; Lester Knight & Associates (1979–85)

This building doesn't look anything like the typical 19th- or even 20th-century government building. Boldly modern, it looks like a giant glass dome with a slice missing from it. Make sure to go inside and look up at the cavernous atrium with its glass elevators.

To compare this modern building with a vastly different style of government building, walk across Randolph to City Hall, built in 1911.

Sears Tower.

to work, shop, dine, and sightsee. From the 103rd-floor Skydeck you can see 50 miles in any direction on a clear day. On a windy day, the top floors sway six inches from true center.

With all the comforts and services available in these skyscrapers, they are kind of like smaller cities within the city of Chicago. One property in Chicago, called Marina City, was specifically designed to function as a self-contained city. Marina City has just about everything you'd find in a typical neighborhood. The two towers, which have been compared to giant corn-cobs setting upright on the north bank of the Chicago River, house condominiums, parking spaces, a grocery store, a movie theater, a fitness center, banks, offices, restaurants, dry cleaners, even a blues club and a bowling alley. For those people who still feel the need to go outside, there's a rooftop deck.

OUT WITH THE OLD

There's only so much room to build in the Chicago's downtown area, so new buildings often replace old ones. This reality often creates conflicts between those who want to preserve existing structures and those who want to demolish and rebuild. This was the case with the Chicago Stock Exchange, an architectural treasure designed by Dankmar Adler and Louis Sullivan. When the owners of the Chicago Stock Exchange announced that they intended to tear down the landmark building, it sparked angry protests in the media and in the streets.

Like many Chicagoans, a preservationist named Richard Nickel believed that such a beautiful and historic building should be preserved. But when the preservationists lost their battle against the wrecking ball, Nickel decided to take it upon himself to save as much of the building as he could. Nickel took many photographs of the Chicago Stock Exchange and also snuck into the building on several nights to scavenge significant artifacts. Tragically, one night the partially dismantled building gave way and Nickel was crushed to death.

The main trading room of the Chicago Stock Exchange was saved from demolition. It was carefully taken apart and then reassembled inside the Art Institute of Chicago, where you can still visit it today.

Preservationists lost the Chicago Stock Exchange battle in 1972, but the dramatic failure served as a wake-up call to the architectural community. During the 1960s and 1970s a number of organizations were created to help prevent the destruction of

Make a Stained Glass Window

Stained glass is an important element in Chicago's architecture. Frank Lloyd Wright included it in many of the homes he designed, and Chicago's houses of worship often feature impressive pieces of glass art. You can experiment with different shapes and patterns to make your own piece of stained glass. For inspiration check out *Chicago Stained Glass* by Erne R. Frueh and Florence Frueh (Loyola Press, 1998), or visit the Smith Museum of Stained Glass at Navy Pier.

YOU'LL NEED

Black marker

5 sheets of plain white paper, 8½ x 11 inches

Colored markers, crayons, or pencils

Ruler

Compass

Plexiglas (available at art supply stores)

12 sheets of construction paper, 8½ x 11 inches, various colors (optional)

Even if you plan to make a piece of Plexiglas stained glass, it's a good idea to experiment on paper first. Use a black marker to draw thick lines on the paper. These lines will represent the lead that holds in place the different pieces of glass in a stained window. These are called *cames*.

You can either use the ruler and compass to make geometric shapes or draw a freehand design. Or try both and see which one you like better. After you finish the dark lines, fill in the various shapes with different colored markers, crayons, or pencils. Stained glass artists often use some pieces of clear glass, so you might want to leave some spaces blank

These three figures show how much a design can change as more lines are added.

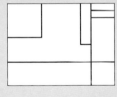 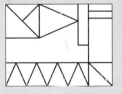

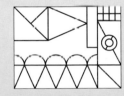

If you prefer, you can try to re-create a piece of stained glass based on a design by someone else. For example, the fourth figure below is based on a detail from a stained glass window in Frank Lloyd Wright's Robie House.

Once you settle on a design you like, place it beneath the Plexiglas and trace it with a black marker. Color in the segments of glass using colored markers. When you're done, place your stained glass near a window to see what it looks like when the light streams through it.

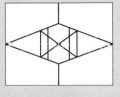

151

Water and Fire

IN THE 1950s Chicago suffered two more tragedies. On June 26, 1954, a giant wave hit the shores of Chicago beaches, sweeping eight people to their deaths. Like a mini tsunami, the wave was a phenomenon called a *seiche*. A far greater tragedy in terms of lives lost occurred in 1958, when a fire broke out in the basement at Our Lady of Angels School on Chicago's West Side. In the third-worst fire in Chicago's history, 92 students and three nuns died.

Chicago's architectural legacy. When the Glessner House in Chicago was threatened with demolition, a group of architects banded together and raised the funds needed to purchase the building. Members of this group eventually became the Chicago Architecture Foundation, whose mission is to educate the public about the value of Chicago's built environment through tours, lectures, and publications. The Landmarks Preservation Council of Illinois is another group active in preserving the state's architectural heritage.

THE RACIAL DIVIDE DEEPENS

The strong postwar economy and the surge in building were the good news in Chicago. The bad news was that racial tensions were again brewing in Chicago. After World War II, African Americans in Chicago again lost their manufacturing jobs to returning white soldiers. And African American soldiers who had defended freedom abroad found few signs of gratitude upon their return.

During the summer of 1955 an African American Chicagoan was the victim of a brutal case of racial violence. A 14-year-old Chicagoan named Emmett Till was visiting his aunt and uncle in the small southern town of Money, Mississippi. One day Emmett and some of his young cousins were buying snacks at a country store. Accounts of what happened in the store differed, but some witnesses claimed Till may have whistled suggestively at Carolyn Bryant, a young married white woman who worked at the store.

Several days later, Till was kidnapped in the middle of the night from his uncle's home by several white men armed with guns. One of the kidnappers was Roy Bryant, husband of the store clerk. Another man was Roy Bryant's half brother, J. W. Milam. The men later admitted kidnapping the boy but told police that they merely questioned Till and then released him. Unfortunately, Till did not return home the next morning.

Two days later, Till's dead body was found in the Tallahatchie River. The boy had been beaten and shot in the head. His body was weighed down by a 150-pound iron farm tool, bound to the boy's body with barbed wire. The story of Till's murder, which was a form of lynching, drew international attention, especially after Till's mother insisted that her son's casket be left open during visitation, in order to show the world "what they did to my son."

Bryant and Milam were arrested and charged with murder. After deliberating for just one hour, an all-white jury found the defendants not guilty. Several months after the trial, Roy Bryant and J. W. Milam were interviewed by *Look* magazine. In the article, the two admitted what many already knew: that they had in fact killed Emmett Till. They claimed that they had only planned to scare the boy, but that they changed their minds when Till refused to be intimidated by his kidnappers.

Fifty years later, federal authorities would reopen the Till case. With Bryant and Milam now deceased, the new investigation focused on trying to find out if any other living individuals had been involved. However, no new charges have yet been filed.

The outrage sparked by Till's lynching was one of the factors that fed the growing civil rights movement. It was only three months later that Rosa Parks was arrested in Montgomery, Alabama, for refusing to give her seat to a white bus passenger.

The Emmett Till case was a reminder to African Americans living up north that they were still not safe from racial violence in the United States. It's true that Chicago's African Americans were not subject to Jim Crow laws, which denied southern African Americans fundamental rights, like voting and equal access to public services. In Chicago, African Americans could vote, they could hold public office, and they were more likely to get government jobs than southern blacks were. As early as 1940, Chicago had an African American police captain. According to the *Encyclopedia of Chicago*, at this time Chicago "was home to the nation's most powerful black politician, Democratic congressman William L. Dawson; the most prominent black man in America, boxing champion Joe Louis; and the most widely read black newspaper, the *Chicago Defender*." The city had also established the Chicago Committee on Racial Equality in 1942 and the Mayor's Committee on Race Relations in 1943.

Of course, African Americans were still discriminated against in Chicago, especially when it came to housing and education. Following World War II, the African American population again doubled, surpassing 800,000 by 1960. Many of these new Chicagoans were poor and many were forced to live in the poorest sections of the city. In an effort to relieve the situation, the Chicago Housing Authority (CHA) recommended the construction of numerous public housing developments throughout the city. But white voters and their aldermen objected, fearing that it would bring more blacks into traditionally white neighborhoods. Instead, the CHA, using federal funds, built rows and rows of high-rise public housing "projects," such as Cabrini-Green, Stateway Gardens, and the Robert Taylor Homes.

Years later, the CHA learned a hard lesson: that it's not a good idea to concentrate so much poverty and despair into one small area. Drugs, crime, and violence were widespread in the projects, dooming them to be a failed social experiment.

Go-Go Sox

IN 1959, the Chicago White Sox won their first American League pennant since the 1919 Black Sox scandal.

Like the Hitless Wonders of 1906, this Sox team was able to score lots of runs on few hits. Known as the Go-Go Sox, they were good at stealing bases and at taking advantage of the opposing team's mistakes. But this team was no group of hitless wonders. American League Most Valuable Player Nellie Fox had a .306 batting average, and Sherm Lollar and Ted Kluszewski were both feared power hitters. Shortstop Luis Aparicio knew how to get on base, and he also led the major leagues that year with 56 stolen bases. White Sox pitcher Early Wynn won the Cy Young award that year with a league best 22–10 record.

Unfortunately, the White Sox would not lift the Black Sox curse, at least not yet. They lost the World Series 4–2 to the Los Angeles Dodgers behind the pitching of Don Drysdale. Kluszewski hit three homers and batted .391 in the series, Fox hit .375, and Aparicio batted .308 in a losing effort.

There were other ways that whites made it hard for blacks to move into white neighborhoods. Some white homeowners refused to sell their homes to blacks. Others were bound by legal contracts (called *restrictive covenants*) that prohibited homeowners in certain neighborhoods from selling their homes to African Americans. Banks and real estate agents also discriminated against African Americans, refusing to provide them with loans for certain homes or steering them toward properties in African American neighborhoods.

Not surprisingly, the schools in the African American ghettos were not as good as the schools in white neighborhoods. The buildings were run down, supplies were scarce, and it was difficult to recruit good teachers to work in these districts.

Discrimination in housing and education would further isolate blacks and whites, while depriving blacks of their rights and opportunities. These problems would worsen over the next few decades and come to a boil in the 1960s.

THE FIRST MAYOR DALEY

In the years after World War II, the Democratic Party continued to strengthen its grasp on political power in Chicago. Since Anton Cermak was elected in 1931, every Chicago mayor has been a Democrat. In 1955 Richard J. Daley was elected mayor of Chicago, a job he held until his death in 1976. Under the leadership of Daley and the Democrats, Chicago experienced a boom in the construction of public buildings, highways, and other municipal improvements. As rail transportation gave way to air transportation O'Hare International Airport was expanded and improved in the early 1960s, replacing Midway International Airport as the world's busiest airport. A third airport,

Meigs Field, was opened on Northerly Island. The rapid building that took place during Daley's first decade in office was capped off in 1965 with the construction of the Chicago Civic Center, later renamed the Daley Center following the mayor's death.

The pace of building continued throughout the second half of the 1960s. According to a history of public works prepared by the city of Chicago, "from 1966–71, total construction exceeded $7.8 billion in Chicago. This figure was the largest for any metropolitan area in the country." Some of the other city projects included improvements made to the water system, as well as to the disposal and treatment of sewage.

Two of Mayor Daley's biggest projects at this time were the construction of the University of Illinois at Chicago campus and the Dan Ryan Expressway. These projects brought a world-class educational institution to the city, improved transportation, and created jobs in the community. But not everyone agreed with the mayor's plans. To make room for the new campus buildings and the expressway, many homes and businesses had to be demolished. The Dan Ryan Expressway also created a dividing line between the mostly white Bridgeport neighborhood to the west and mostly black Englewood neighborhood to the east.

A young Richard J. Daley (1902–1976) campaigned on horseback in the 1955 mayoral election.

Daley obviously knew how to get things done. For many years he was able to preserve social order and gain personal power through the political system. Daley was like the all-powerful Wizard of Oz, pulling levers and orchestrating the city's events from behind the curtain of his City Hall office. By doling out jobs and government services to friends or in return for favors, Daley was able to gain allies that helped him win election after election. Chicago's well-oiled political system came to be known as "the machine."

In the mid- and late 1960s, Daley's machine encountered new opponents. The civil rights and anti-war movements were being propelled by people who didn't have a say in government. African Americans and younger members of society felt like their interests weren't being represented by elected officials. So they took to the streets and attempted to apply pressure on Chicago's government through protests, boycotts, and other confrontational methods.

For years, African Americans in Chicago had been trying to increase their access to quality schools and housing. But they made little progress. In 1966 Dr. Martin Luther King Jr. decided to come to Chicago to help local civil rights leaders, such as Al Raby, Dick Gregory, and Jesse Jackson. Focusing on housing issues, King moved into a run-down West Side apartment building to show just how bad living conditions were for most African Americans living in Chicago. He also gave speeches, led marches, and challenged Mayor Daley to improve the situation.

King succeeded in bringing more attention to the issues, but little changed in the long run. Daley refused to let King make him look like the enemy of civil rights. He publicly welcomed King to Chicago and pledged to work with King to rid the city of poverty. But Daley's

reforms were minor and had little lasting impact. As long as African Americans were living in poor neighborhoods with bad roads, schools, parks, and homes, they would never be able to achieve equality.

When Dr. Martin Luther King Jr. was assassinated on April 4, 1968, riots broke out in many major American cities, including Chicago. It was during these riots that Daley uttered his most notorious remarks. He ordered his police officers to "shoot to kill any arsonist or anyone with a Molotov cocktail in his hand in Chicago because they're potential murderers." These comments further divided the white and black communities in Chicago, making race relations even more difficult in the coming years.

The city restored order but only temporarily. In August, the national Democratic Party held its convention in Chicago. The purpose of the convention was to nominate a candidate for the presidential election, but the event also served as a stage for protest among Democrats who felt betrayed by their party. Many voters—especially younger members of society—were against the country's involvement in the Vietnam War. They hoped the Democratic Party would nominate a presidential candidate who would promise to pull the United States out of the war.

Police spraying a newspaper photographer during the 1968 Democratic National Convention riots in downtown Chicago.

Protesters mocking National Guardsmen during the 1968 Democratic National Convention riots in downtown Chicago.

But for the most part these people did not have any voice in the Democratic Party. So they used tactics like public protest: marches, sit-ins, public speeches, and so on. Two leaders of the Youth International Party, or Yippies, Abbie Hoffman and Jerry Rubin, were especially good at creating spectacles that would get the attention of the media. They made outrageous claims that were more intended to upset the establishment than they were serious. For instance, Hoffman claimed to be masterminding a plot to de-pants Hubert Humphrey, a candidate for the presidential nomination, at the convention.

Daley had no patience with these kinds of antics. Like many older and more conservative Chicagoans, he described the protesters as disrespectful, troublemaking hippies who should stay out of Chicago and mind their own business. But if he was unable to keep protest groups from coming to Chicago, he would at least try to keep them away from the convention. To do so, Daley set up elaborate security measures. With thousands of police officers, FBI, and Secret Service agents, as well as army troops mobilized, Chicago looked and felt more like a war zone.

Just like when the Chicago Fire occurred in 1871, all the conditions for disaster were present in the summer of 1968. All that was needed was a spark, which was provided by the Chicago Police Department. On several occasions, the police attacked peaceful crowds of demonstrators, beating them with night sticks. And they also attacked innocent bystanders as well as journalists reporting the events. No other news reporter was more trusted at this time than Walter Cronkite. Complaining about the violence he witnessed, Cronkite said, "I want to pack my bags and get out of this city."

With scenes of blatant police brutality broadcast for all to see on the television news, the Democratic National Convention

Richard J. Daley in his later years.

The Chicago Seven

A FEDERAL COMMISSION established to investigate the convention violence squarely pointed the finger at the police and Mayor Daley's administration. Even so, a handful of the demonstrators were still put on trial for planning and causing the violence. The trial of Abbie Hoffman, Jerry Rubin, Tom Hayden, and four others was as much of a farce as the Yippie demonstrations. In the end, all were cleared of charges.

became an international embarrassment for Mayor Daley. Defending the police, Daley made his most famous verbal slip: "The policeman isn't there to create disorder. The policeman is there to preserve disorder." He meant to say "preserve order," but some people have said that Daley's statement was accidentally more accurate than he would have admitted.

A year and a half later another case of police brutality marked a low point in relations between city government and the African American community in Chicago. In 1968 a group of African Americans had started the Chicago chapter of the Black Panther Party, a nationwide "black power" organization. The leader of Chicago's Black Panthers was Fred Hampton. Where civil rights leaders like Dr. Martin Luther King Jr. used peaceful methods, the Black Panthers took a more militant stance. Objecting to police brutality, poverty, and segregation, Hampton sometimes said things in the media that got the attention of the authorities, such as, "Pick up your guns and fight the pigs." But Hampton was a local hero in his West Side neighborhood for organizing free food programs for poor children.

On December 4, 1969, Chicago police stormed Hampton's apartment in the middle of the night. The police said that the Black Panthers shot at them as they entered the apartment, and that police only returned fire in self-defense. However, testimony and physical evidence told a different story. It appears that Hampton was shot while lying in bed. Hampton and one other member of the Black Panthers, Mark Clark, died in the raid, and four others received gunshot wounds. Two police officers received minor injuries. Investigators found almost 100 bullets at the scene. Only one of them was fired from a Black Panther gun, but no one knows who pulled the trigger.

The Richard J. Daley era came to an end on December 20, 1976, when he died of a heart attack. Whether they loved him or hated him, many Chicagoans agreed that Daley had been an incredibly powerful and influential mayor. During his time in office, Chicago underwent many of the changes that continue to make it a great city—a center for commerce, transportation, and culture. On the other hand, Daley's legacy will also be remembered as a time in which racial divisions and inequalities were unfortunately reinforced.

Maybe the best indication of Daley's power and weaknesses was seen in the following years, as City Hall struggled and foundered without the guidance of a strong leader.

From a Billy Goat to a Black Cat

THE CHICAGO CUBS looked like they were the team to beat in 1969. They raced to an 11–1 record at the beginning of the season. And by the time starting pitcher Kenny Holtzman threw a no-hitter on August 19 the Cubs held a commanding 7 ½-game lead over the New York Mets. But things took a turn for the worse after that. The Mets made a late-season charge as the Cubs began to falter. On September 10, 1969, the Mets beat the Cubs 7–1 to complete a series sweep and reduce the Cubs lead to a half game. This was the infamous game in which a black cat appeared on the baseball field and walked past the Cubs dugout, adding a new chapter to the Cubs long history of near misses and self-destruction. And it wouldn't be the final chapter either.

12
Chicago in the New Millennium

Time Line

1979 Jane Byrne elected first female mayor of Chicago

1980 Chicago hires its first female firefighters

1983 Harold Washington elected first African American mayor of Chicago

1984 Chicago hosts its first annual Blues Festival

1986 The Chicago Bears win Super Bowl XX

1987 Chicago Public Schools declared nation's worst

1989 Navy Pier reopens after $150 million renovation; Chicago Children's Museum moves to Navy Pier

1990 Old Comiskey Park demolished

1991 Chicago Bulls win first NBA championship

1992 Great Chicago Flood

1995 Heat wave claims over 739 lives; Ferris wheel added to Navy Pier

1996 Chicago Housing Authority begins demolition of high-rise public housing

2004 Millennium Park opens

2005 White Sox win World Series

2006 Chicago Historical Society celebrates its 150th anniversary, opens the newly remodeled and renamed Chicago History Museum

RICHARD J. DALEY had been the mayor for so long—21 years—that without him the city of Chicago seemed lost and aimless. For better or worse, Daley had ruled the city of Chicago like it was his personal kingdom. The only problem was that he failed to appoint a successor to the throne before his death.

In the next 13 years Chicago had six different mayors and plenty of turmoil. On the bright side, the city elected its first woman mayor, Jane Byrne, in 1979, and its first African American mayor, Harold Washington, in 1983.

This 2004 photograph of Millennium Park shows the Crown Fountain in the foreground, Cloud Gate to the left, and the Jay Pritzker Pavilion in the background.

PHOTO BY TERRY EVANS, *REVEALING CHICAGO*

The first mayor after Richard J. Daley was Michael Bilandic, who later became the first Chicago mayor to ever lose an election to a snowstorm. Well, sort of. The blizzard of 1979 dumped 20 inches of snow on Chicago over the weekend of January 12–14. It snowed several more times in the month, bringing the total amount of snow on the ground to 47 inches by the end of January. The overwhelming snowfall basically shut the city down for about a month. CTA trains got stuck in the snow or broke down trying to plow through it. People couldn't get to work. Also, garbage trucks couldn't get through the snow-clogged alleys, so garbage started piling up, attracting rats. Obviously, the storm wasn't Bilandic's fault, but how the city handled the crisis was.

The storm couldn't have come at a worse time for Bilandic—or at a better time for his challenger, Jane Byrne. A former supporter of Richard J. Daley, Byrne had been fired from her city job in 1977 when Bilandic took over the mayor's office. Byrne cleverly took advantage of the snowstorm. She told newspaper and television reporters that the poor response to the blizzard was a perfect example of how disorganized and ineffective Bilandic was. Her strategy worked. Byrne got more votes than Bilandic to win the Democratic Party primary. In the general

New Era of Racial Politics

ONE OF THE REASONS for the political chaos in Chicago in the late 1970s and into the 1980s was that many long-standing political relationships died with Richard J. Daley. For years Daley had supported Alderman William Dawson, an African American who represented a South Side ward. Dawson delivered votes to Daley, Daley delivered jobs and services to Dawson's ward. Dawson died in 1970, and Daley died in 1976. The people who took over for them did not develop the same kind of relationships.

election Byrne easily beat the Republican candidate Wallace Johnson to become the city's first female mayor.

It turned out that Byrne had an easier time winning an election than running a city. For one thing, she was now in charge of the same government that she had criticized so harshly during her campaign. CTA workers, public school teachers, and firefighters all held strikes during Byrne's term as mayor, hurting Byrne's popularity. Byrne also made several decisions that angered members of Chicago's African American community. For example, in 1981 Byrne and her husband moved into a Cabrini-Green public housing unit, which was mostly occupied by African Americans. By moving into the crime-ridden housing projects, she tried to show that she understood her citizen's problems and that she would take the necessary steps to

fix them. Police protection was of course improved for the three weeks Byrne lived in Cabrini-Green, but things went back to the way they were as soon as she left.

When the next election came around, African Americans in Chicago rallied around black candidate Harold Washington. In the Democratic primary election in 1983, Washington was up against Mayor Byrne and Richard M. Daley, son of former mayor Richard J. Daley. Washington won the primary election and should have been a shoo-in for mayor. Ever since the 1930s the candidate who won the Democratic primary was a sure winner for the general election. But in one of the most shameful moments in Chicago's racial politics, a majority of white Democratic voters switched sides. Rather than vote for a black Democratic candidate, they voted for the white Republican candidate Bernard Epton. But it didn't work, thanks mostly to a large-scale effort to encourage Chicago's African Americans to vote.

Winning the election was only half the battle. Chicago's first black mayor, Harold Washington, now faced serious opposition in the Chicago City Council, which is the city's version of the legislative branch. A majority of the white aldermen banded together to oppose Washington's plans. They also prevented him from doing what every Chicago mayor had always done: give government jobs to people who helped him win the election. If Washington couldn't give the jobs to whom he wanted, he would get rid of the jobs altogether. Washington cut 10,000 jobs from the city payroll—jobs held mostly by white city workers who had

Harold Washington (1922–1987) takes the oath of office in 1983 to become Chicago's first African American mayor.

AS PUBLISHED IN THE CHICAGO SUN-TIMES ON APRIL 29, 1983. COPYRIGHT © 2008 BY CHICAGO SUN TIMES, INC. REPRINTED WITH PERMISSION. PHOTOGRAPHER: KEITH HALE.

Chicago's Racial Mix

White 42%

African American 36%

Hispanic 26%

Asian 4%

Source: U.S. Census, 2000

been hired during the Daley, Bilandic, and Byrne years.

With all the fighting between the mayor's office and the City Council, this period of Chicago's government history is referred to as "Council Wars." Things changed after the 1986 elections, when Washington's allies won enough seats in the City Council to get

a majority of the votes. Washington didn't have much time to take advantage of his new position, however. He died of a heart attack on November 25, 1987. Alderman David Orr served as interim mayor for a short time. Then Eugene Sawyer was appointed mayor by the City Council, becoming Chicago's second African

American mayor. Two years later Richard M. Daley won the mayoral election.

Although the second Daley's style differs from his father's, there are some things about this Mayor Daley that are very similar to the first Mayor Daley. They both believed in big building projects. To attract business conventions to Chicago, a number of new buildings have been added to the McCormick Place convention center. A major renovation of Navy Pier (1989) and the construction of Millennium Park (2004) have created two of Chicago's most popular recreation spaces, attracting tourists from around the world and bringing people from all parts of Chicagoland into the downtown area.

Mayor Daley has also shown an interest in enhancing the beauty of the city. Planting thousands of trees and flowers in parks and along streets, Mayor Daley has succeeded in making Chicago a "greener" city.

SUMMERTIME BLUES

When people think about original music from Chicago, they think about the blues. What better way to celebrate Chicago's contribution to a unique American art form than with a party? In 1984 the city hosted its first annual Chicago Blues Festival in Grant Park. Every year since, the Chicago

Muddy Waters was an influential blues entertainer who helped make Chicago the blues capital of the world.
PHOTO BY PAUL NATKIN

Blues Festival has been the largest and most popular of Chicago's summer music festivals, drawing up to three quarters of a million spectators over four days of music, food, and camaraderie.

The blues may have been born in the Deep South, but they grew up in Chicago. Some of the earliest Chicago blues musicians were actually performing their craft back in the early 1920s when jazz was at the top of Chicago's music scene. Chicago blues really hit its stride in the 1950s, when artists like Muddy Waters, Willie Dixon, and Howlin' Wolf were Chicago's blues stars. At this time, on Chicago's south and west sides there were many venues where blues artists could perform. Many of these musicians also recorded their songs with local recording studios, such as Chess Records and Vee-Jay Records.

In the 1960s and 1970s, the new generation of blues performers included musicians such as Buddy Guy, Junior Wells, and Otis Rush. Some of the legendary blues clubs have shut down over the years, but others

Interview with the Queen of the Blues

CHICAGOAN Koko Taylor, the "Queen of the Blues," provides expert advice and tips on the art of blues songwriting.

Can anybody write a blues song?

Anybody who wants to. It don't matter how old you are or anything like that. All that matters is if you want to do it and that you try hard enough. It takes a lot of hard work. I don't want nobody to think this is easy.

Koko Taylor.
COURTESY OF ALLIGATOR RECORDS

Does a blues song have to be sad?

No. I don't know why people say that. I'm working on recording a new CD right now. And I got I think seven songs on this CD that I wrote and ain't none of them sad. The blues don't have to be sad, they should make you happy. When you're writing a blues song, you think happy thoughts. You think good thoughts, just like if you were writing a jazz song, or a rock-and-roll song, or whatever. The blues is only a name for a style of music.

Okay, so if a person wants to write a blues song, how would they go about it?

Well, what I do is this. First I start thinking about what I want to say.

Then I might come up with one word or phrase, maybe something like:

I love you, baby.

Now, don't nobody know what that means. And sometime I don't know myself. So, now we need to add to that. Then a day later, I might have thought of something else to go with that. I might say:

I love you baby, like a dog loves his bone.

Now, that's a good start, but a blues song has to tell a story, and it has to rhyme. So now I think of words that rhyme with bone. After a while I'll find a word that rhymes and also makes sense. Then I might add the next line:

I love you baby, like a dog loves his bone.
And I want everybody to leave my thing alone.

And that's how I come up with a blues song. I start with something small and keep adding word by word. If I come up with some that don't sound right, then I erase that from my mind, until I think of something else. And I just keep putting words together until I come up with a complete song.

Some people might try to sit down with pen and paper or at the computer and write a song straight through.

No, no, no. That's not how it works. I done wrote a lot of songs, and I don't come up with a song like poppin' your fingers. It's not that simple. It might take me a month, it might take me a week. But there were times when I wrote a song in one day. It clicked just like that. Sometimes it comes right out, sometimes it won't. You never know.

Write Your Own Blues Song

Like many types of writing, the trick to writing a blues song is to start simple and add little by little. Then you can think about what you have and keep the things you like and get rid of the things you don't like (that's called editing). Keep in mind that a blues song doesn't have to be sad. It might even end up being kind of silly, like "Spinach for Dinner Blues."

You can use many of the same techniques discussed in the poetry-writing activity in chapter 10. But in this case you may also want to pay special attention to the rhythm of the words. To give you an example, here is a portion of the lyrics to a blues song written in 1921. It describes the often thankless job of the porters who worked on Pullman railroad cars.

"PULLMAN PORTER BLUES"
By Clifford Ulrich and Burton Hamilton

I feel oh so blue,
I really don't know what to do.
I got a brand new job—a tip collector,
It's some job, a car protector,
Since I left my home and started on railroads
  to roam,
I get nothing but abuse,
So tell me what's the use.

It's "Pullman Porter, draft on my feet."
It's "Pullman Porter, turn on the heat."
It's "Pullman Porter," all live-long day.
"Pullman Porter bring me water," that's all
  they say,
It's "Pullman Porter, make up my berth."
It's "Pullman Porter no place on earth,"
"Oh Pullman Porter, won't you shine my shoes,"
I got the Pullman Porter Blues.

opened in their place, including several clubs on Chicago's North Side, such as Kingston Mines, Rosa's Lounge, and B.L.U.E.S.

Chess Records went out of business in 1975, but newcomer Alligator Records, founded in 1971, picked up where Chess left off, recording the music of living legends Koko Taylor and Lonnie Brooks.

DA BEARS

Although running back Walter Payton had been setting and breaking NFL records for the Bears since he first joined the team in

Third City

LATE IN THE 20th century, Chicago lost its claim to being the "second city," as Los Angeles surpassed Chicago in population.

New York   8,008,278 (city)
              9,314,235 (metro)

Los Angeles   3,694,820 (city)
              9,519,338 (metro)

Chicago   2,896,016 (city)
              8,272,768 (metro)

Source: U.S. Census, 2000

1975, the team had nothing to show for it. Their last NFL championship was back in 1963, and they had never won a Super Bowl. Still, fans loved to watch Payton run past—and sometimes over—opposing teams, especially on November 20, 1977, when he gained a then-record 275 yards against the Minnesota Vikings. But Payton was never satisfied with individual records. He wanted his team to win it all.

In 1985, a combination of talent and personality made the Chicago Bears a special team that no Bears fan of that era will ever forget. Middle linebacker Mike Singletary was the on-field brains and spirit of the Bears defense. The Bears also had what may have been the best defensive line ever, with William "Refrigerator" Perry, Dan Hampton, Richard Dent, and Steve McMichael. On the offensive side, the Bears added Jim McMahon, a quarterback with a strong and accurate throwing arm, as well as speedy receivers Dennis McKinnon and former Olympic sprinter Willie Gault. Of course, Payton was still in the backfield, joined by Matt Suhey, along with a new offensive weapon. In one of the most bizarre moves in football history, head coach Mike Ditka took to using the 300-pound "Refrigerator" Perry as a running back in goal-line situations. At first, Perry would provide lead blocking for Walter Payton, but later in the season, the Fridge carried the ball for two touchdowns and even caught a pass for a touchdown.

The Bears went 15–1 in that season and won Super Bowl XX by a score of 46–10. It was the perfect final chapter in Payton's career. In all, he rushed for 16,726 yards, reaching the 100-yard mark in 77 games. Perhaps most astoundingly, Payton missed only one game in his 13-year career. His conditioning and strength were legendary.

Considering Payton's accomplishments and his physical powers, it was all the more shocking and sad when he became ill at a young age. In 1999 Payton died of a rare liver disease at the age of 45. His memory lives on in his records, as well as in the hearts of football teammates and fans. Chicago also named Walter Payton College Prep high school in Payton's honor.

DA BULLS

For years Walter Payton provided all the thrills for Bears fans, as the rest of his team underachieved. In the 1980s the Chicago Bulls got their basketball version of Payton in the form of Michael Jordan, who became what many consider the best player in the history of basketball.

Heat Wave

IN EARLY JULY 1995 the city's weather reporters were predicting an unusually bad heat wave. When temperatures reached 106 degrees on July 13, 1995, Chicago residents cranked up the air conditioning. The demands on electricity caused power outages. People without power, and others who never had air conditioners in the first place, may have felt like they were living in an oven. With a heat index of 126 degrees, people did whatever they could to get relief. People flocked to the beaches or to playgrounds with fountains. At other locations the fire department turned on their hoses and sprayed people to cool them off.

Hospitals were overwhelmed with people suffering from heat stroke and other conditions made worse by the high temperatures. Ambulances, which typically respond in minutes, were running hours behind schedule.

The final death toll for the week reached 735. The city has since set up a system to warn vulnerable citizens when the National Weather Service issues a Heat Warning or a Wind Chill Warning.

Jordan made it clear in his rookie season that he would be a force in the NBA, scoring 28 points per game on his way to being named Rookie of the Year and being voted to the All Star team. But the team still ended the season with a losing record. Jordan broke his foot during his second season and ended up playing only 18 games. But the Bulls still made it into the playoffs, which gave Jordan the opportunity to show off on a national stage. He scored a record-setting 63 points in game two against the Celtics, but the Bulls still lost that game and the series, bowing out in the first round.

In the 1986–87 season, the team improved its record and again made the playoffs, where they lost in the first round. Injury-free that year, Michael Jordan led the league in scoring (3,041 points) and in points per game (37.1).

But what good are individual awards and records if your team is losing? Not even Michael Jordan could do it alone. Bulls management added new players Horace Grant, Scottie Pippen, Bill Cartwright, and Craig Hodges. Over the next two years the Bulls not only made the playoffs but also won the first two playoff series each year. But both times they lost the Eastern Conference Final to their archrivals, the Detroit Pistons.

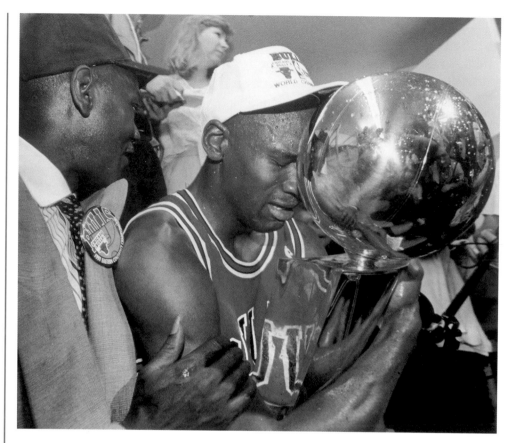

Michael Jordan is overcome with emotion after winning his first NBA championship in 1991.

Things were different in 1990–91. The Bulls, led by new head coach Phil Jackson, beat the Pistons to make it to their first NBA final series. They lost game one to the Los Angeles Lakers, but swept the series after that, winning their first NBA championship.

Two more championships followed before Jordan surprised Chicago and the world by announcing his retirement from basketball.

The Bulls played well in Jordan's absence but failed to take home the NBA trophy in the next two years. Meanwhile

Jordan struggled to hit curveballs as an outfielder on a White Sox minor league team. Jordan hung up his baseball mitt and returned to the Bulls late in the 1994–95 season, but Jordan and Pippen's heroics were not enough. The Bulls fell to the Orlando Magic in the playoffs.

The following year the Bulls got it back together, winning an NBA record 72 games out of 82. Jordan and Pippen were joined by center Luc Longley, rebounding and defensive specialist Dennis Rodman, and shooting guard Steve Kerr. The Bulls won the NBA championship trophy again that year, beginning their second "three-peat"— three straight NBA titles.

But all good things must come to an end. Phil Jackson, Michael Jordan, Scottie Pippen, and Dennis Rodman all left the Bulls after the team's last NBA title in the 1997–98 season. Without the stars that made the 1990s a decade to remember for Bulls fans, the team has yet to perform well enough to come close to another championship.

BLACK SOX NO MORE

The Chicago White Sox had experienced their own problems. The Sox had not made it to the World Series since 1959, and hadn't won it since 1917. Some fans had to wonder if the South Siders were forever doomed to pay for the 1919 Black Sox scandal, in which the team deliberately threw the World Series in order to win bets placed on the Cincinnati Reds.

In 2005 the Chicago White Sox proved that a Chicago baseball team could once again win the World Series. Under manager Ozzie Guillen, the Sox led the majors through most of the season. Behind the dominant pitching of Mark Buehrle, Jose Contreras, Jon Garland, and Freddy Garcia, the Sox finished the season with a record of 99–63. Solid fielding, teamwork, and hustle were the hallmarks of the White Sox success. The Sox continued to get strong pitching in the

White Sox players celebrate after winning the 2005 World Series over the Houston Astros on October 26, 2005.
RONALD MARTINEZ/GETTY IMAGES

Great Chicago Flood

THE LOOP'S UNDERGROUND tunnel flood of 1992 will go down as one of the city's most expensive and avoidable disasters. Late in 1991 the city hired the Great Lakes Dredge & Dock Company to replace some rotting wooden pilings in the Chicago River. But what the employees drilling the new holes didn't know was that beneath the Chicago River there was an old freight tunnel. The drill punctured a small hole in one of the tunnel walls. What started as a slow leak turned into a massive flood when the wall gave way in April 1992.

Dug in the late 1800s, the 60-mile network of tunnels was originally used to shuttle coal to downtown buildings. More recently, the tunnels were used for electrical and communications wiring.

As 250 million gallons of water poured through the pierced tunnel, a small whirlpool became visible on the surface of the Chicago River. Basements throughout the Loop were filled with water, knocking out electricity and phone lines, causing massive amounts of property damage, and closing businesses down for weeks.

By the time all the water was pumped out and things were back to normal, the losses from property damage and lost business added up to $1 billion.

postseason, along with the power hitting of first baseman Paul Konerko and timely clutch hitting from third baseman Joe Crede. The Sox swept the Boston Red Sox in the Division Series, then beat the Los Angeles Angels of Anaheim to take the pennant.

The Chicago White Sox ended 88 years of disappointment when they triumphed over the Houston Astros to win the 2005 Major League Baseball World Series. The Sox swept the Astros in four games, capping an amazing postseason record of 11–1.

LOVABLE LOSERS NO MORE?

In 2004 and 2005 the World Series was won by teams with the third (Boston Red Sox) and second (Chicago White Sox) longest losing streaks in baseball. Guess who still has the longest streak of seasons without winning a World Series? That's right, the Chicago Cubs, who haven't won a World Series since 1908.

The Cubs have had their share of great position players, like Ernie Banks, Billy Williams, Ron Santo, Ryne Sandberg and Sammy Sosa. Chicago also had great pitchers over the years, such as Cy Young award winners Ferguson Jenkins (1971), Bruce Sutter (1979), Rick Sutcliffe (1984), and Greg Maddux (1992). Cub pitchers have thrown six no-hitters since 1955, with Ken Holtzman accounting for two of them, in 1969 and 1971.

There have also been great Cubs teams, but they've never been able to get back to the World Series. The 1969 team looked like a shoo-in to win the pennant but somehow surrendered first place to a late-season charge by the New York Mets. In 1984 and 1989 the Cubs made it to the playoffs, but lost.

But those disappointments are nothing compared to the disastrous conclusion of the 2003 season. The Cubs had just won their first postseason series in 95 years, and all they had to do to get into the World Series was beat the Florida Marlins in the National League Championship Series. The Cubs led the series 3–2. Leading game 6 3–0, the Cubs were just five outs away from a World Series. But the Cubs curse again reared its ugly head. A Marlins batter hit a lazy foul ball toward the wall in shallow left field. Left fielder Moises Alou jumped to catch the ball, but it was deflected by a Cubs fan. Given a second chance, the Marlins rallied to win the game 8–3. Instead of going on to the World Series, the Cubs were forced to play a decisive game 7, which they lost to the Marlins, who went on to win the World Series. Once again the Cubs found a way to lose.

But now that the Red Sox and White Sox have reversed their curses, will it be the Cubs' turn to win the World Series? Or will their curse prove the most enduring one of all? Only time will tell whether or not Cubs fans can ever finish a season without having to repeat that eternal refrain: "Wait 'til next year."

END OF THE LINE

With the loss of several famous Chicago businesses, the first few years of the 21st century have been hard on names that have figured prominently in Chicago's history. In 2002 the highly respected accounting firm Arthur Andersen fell victim to a lawsuit related to the collapse of an energy company called Enron. A criminal conviction of Arthur Andersen was later overruled in appeals court, but the damage to the company's reputation was already done. Having lost its clients as well as its international partners, the 89-year-old accounting firm all but went out of business in 2002.

Since 1881 shoppers in Chicago could rely on the service and high-quality products being offered under the name of Marshall Field & Company. Chicago's premier department store didn't go out of business, but it was renamed by its corporate parent.

All-time Cub greats, Billy Williams (left) and Ernie Banks (right), pose with a young fan before a home game in 1972.
COURTESY OF GREGORY BEZKOROVAINY

Make a Chicago-Style Hot Dog

Chicago is known as the City of Big Shoulders, but with its love of fatty foods, it could also be called the City of Big Bellies. Much of the blame can be placed on Chicago-style hot dogs, pizza, and Italian beef sandwiches. In just about every corner of the city you can find a variation of the recipe below. But one thing is true for all Chicago-style hot dogs: hold the ketchup!

INGREDIENTS

All-beef hot dog
Poppy seed bun
Pickle slice
Bright green pickle relish
Tomato wedges
Cucumber slices
Yellow mustard
Sport peppers (optional)
Celery salt (optional)

On a stove, bring four cups of water to boil in a medium-sized pot. Place the hot dog into the water, cover, and turn off the heat. After five minutes, remove the hot dog with tongs and place into a bun. Garnish with the ingredients listed above. Keep plenty of napkins handy, and watch out for falling ingredients as you bite into this messy treat.

As of September 2006, the store is now known as Macy's.

Progress is progress, and business is business. So it should come as no surprise when fond memories lose out to economic realities. But a great city like Chicago moves on, celebrating its past, even as the old traditions give way to new developments. Without boldness and innovation, Chicago never would have become the great city it is and will be in the future.

CITY OF NEIGHBORHOODS

Since its earliest days, Chicago has been a melting pot of different ethnic groups and nationalities. The area's first long-term settler was of course, Jean Baptiste Point Du Sable, a black fur trader who set up a farm and trading post on the banks of the Chicago River back in 1782. When the city was chartered in 1837, Chicago was populated by Native Americans who stayed behind after the Potawatomi and other tribes headed west toward reservations in what would later become Oklahoma. Chicago was also home to people from France and the British Isles, as well as many American citizens from the east and south.

Significant numbers of Irish immigrants were lured to Chicago in the 1830s to help build the Illinois & Michigan Canal. A second wave of Irish fleeing the Great Potato Famine descended on Chicago in the late 1840s. During the mid and late 1800s large numbers of Swedes, Russians, Czechs, Poles, Germans, Italians, and other European groups immigrated to Chicago.

About a half million African Americans moved north to Chicago during the Great Migration, from 1916 to 1970. Mexicans had been living in Chicago since the 1910s, but their numbers were more modest until recently. In the 1960s, there were still fewer than 60,000 Mexicans living in Chicago. As of 2000 the Mexican population jumped to more than half a million in Chicago, with another half million in the surrounding suburbs. Migration from Central and South American countries has added to Chicago's Hispanic population.

Asian immigration has been more sporadic. In the late 1800s, small numbers of Chinese and Japanese came to Chicago, but immigration restrictions kept the Asian population relatively low. The Japanese population in Chicago actually grew during World War II, as Japanese were released from internment camps and permitted to work in urban factories to help fill wartime labor shortages. More recently, Chicago has experienced a greater influx of Asian immigrants including Indians, Pakistanis, Vietnamese, Cambodians, Koreans, Laotians, and Thai.

Today Chicago's population includes people from all corners of the world. Take a walk just about anywhere in the city of Chicago and before you've traveled eight blocks you may have experienced as many cultures, if not more. If you return several years later, you may notice a thoroughly different neighborhood vibe. Where Pilsen was once home mostly to Czech immigrants, it has more recently become a predominantly Mexican neighborhood. Andersonville still shows signs of its Swedish character, but many of the departing Swedes have been replaced by a diverse population of different ethnicities and religions, as well as a growing gay and lesbian community.

Usually communities that leave a neighborhood do so gradually. This was the case, for example, with at least one of Chicago's Polish neighborhoods. Dating back to the 1880s many Poles were living on the near northwest side, in a neighborhood sometimes called Polonia. Over the years, many of these Poles have moved northwest along the corridor surrounding Milwaukee Avenue. A population of Poles remains in the area, but now shares the neighborhood with Ukrainians, Hispanics, and African Americans.

There have been some instances when communities have relocated as a group. Chicago's first Chinatown had been within the Loop since the 1880s. In 1910 many of the residents moved to the current Chinatown location on the near South Side (22nd and Wentworth). Still, throughout Chicago's history many Chinese Americans have lived in neighborhoods throughout the city. More recently a second Asian neighborhood has sprung up on the North Side near Chicago's Uptown neighborhood. Beginning in the 1970s, Chinese, Vietnamese, Cambodians, and Laotians have congregated in the area surrounding Argyle Street, from Broadway to Sheridan.

MILLENNIUM PARK

Having considered Chicago's past, it might now be fitting to consider Chicago's most recent and grandiose public building project. Opened in 2004, Millennium Park was built using a formula familiar to Chicago: a combination of public and private funds. Chicago has always been home to citizens with the means and the vision to produce structures and to host events that are larger and more magnificent than they would otherwise be. Like the individuals who invested their time, money, and intellectual capital

into the 1893 and 1933 World's Fairs, and like the benefactors who helped launch and sustain institutions, such as the Field Museum, John G. Shedd Aquarium, Art Institute of Chicago, and Museum of Science and Industry—Chicagoans are too proud to fail, especially on such a grand scale and with so many eyes watching.

So even though the price tag skyrocketed from $150 million to $475 million, even though the deadlines slipped, and even though the grumbling grew louder, the final product has met with local and international praise. Millennium Park is a 24-acre park, garden, and concert venue, with several examples of world-class architecture and sculpture. The most popular attractions are the Pritzker Pavilion with its trellised sound system, the Cloud Gate sculpture, commonly known as "the Bean," and the Crown Fountain with its 50-foot-high towers, which project images reflecting Chicago's multicultural nature.

All in all Millennium Park provides a majestic finishing touch to Chicago's Grant Park, with its more classically designed Buckingham Fountain, gardens, and walking paths. It harkens back to a spirit of civic pride that underlies many of Chicago's finest moments and represents a renewed dedication to Chicago's motto: "I Will."

Resources

KOESTER & ZANDER
KOESTER & ZANDER
THE CUNARD LINE

GOODFRIEND SH

ELSTON AV

BIBLIOGRAPHY

Addams, Jane. *Twenty Years at Hull-House.* New York: Signet Classics, 1999.

Andreas, A. T. *A History of Chicago.* 3 vols. New York: Arno Press, 1975.

Asbury, Herbert. *Gem of the Prairie: An Informal History of the Chicago Underworld.* DeKalb: Northern Illinois University Press, 1986.

Billington, Charles. *Wrigley Field's Last World Series: The Wartime Chicago Cubs and the Pennant of 1945.* Chicago: Lake Claremont Press, 2005.

Bernstein, Arnie. *The Hoofs and Guns of the Storm: Chicago's Civil War Connections.* Chicago: Lake Claremont Press, 2003.

Bonansinga, Jay. *The Sinking of the Eastland.* New York: Citadel Press, 2004.

Brandt, Nat. *Chicago Death Trap: The Iroquois Theatre Fire of 1903.* Carbondale: Southern Illinois University Press, 2003.

Cohen, Adam, and Elizabeth Taylor. *American Pharaoh: Mayor Richard J. Daley: His Battle for Chicago and the Nation.* Boston: Little, Brown, 2000.

Greenberg, Joel. *A Natural History of the Chicago Region.* Chicago: University of Chicago Press, 2002.

Grossman, James. *The Encyclopedia of Chicago.* Chicago: University of Chicago Press, 2004.

Holland, Robert. *Chicago in Maps: 1612–2002.* New York: Rizzoli, 2005.

Karamanski, Theodore J. *Rally 'Round the Flag: Chicago and the Civil War.* Chicago: Nelson Hall Publishers, 1993.

Kitt Chappell, Sally A. *Cahokia: Mirror of the Cosmos.* Chicago: University of Chicago Press, 2002.

Lawlor, Laurie. *Exploring the Chicago World's Fair, 1893.* New York: Aladdin, 2002.

*Lorenz, Albert. *Journey to Cahokia: A Boy's Visit to the Great Mound City.* New York: Abrams, 2004.

Lowe, David. *Lost Chicago.* New York: Watson-Guptill, 2005.

Miller, Donald. *City of the Century: The Epic of Chicago and the Making of America.* New York: Simon & Schuster, 1997.

*Murphy, Jim. *The Great Fire.* New York: Scholastic, 1995.

Pierce, Bessie Louise. *A History of Chicago.* 3 vols. Chicago: University of Chicago Press, 2006.

Pierce, Bessie Louise. *As Others See Chicago: Impressions of Visitors, 1673-1933.* Chicago: University of Chicago Press, 2004.

Struever, Stuart. *Koster: Americans in Search of Their Prehistoric Past.* Long Grove, IL: Waveland Press, 2000.

*Thorne-Thomsen, Kathleen. *Frank Lloyd Wright for Kids: His Life and Ideas, 21 Activites.* Chicago: Chicago Review Press, 1994.

*Tilley Turner, Glennette. *The Underground Railroad in Illinois.* Glen Ellyn: Newman Educational Publishing, 2001.

*Books especially appropriate for readers nine years and older.

PLACES TO VISIT

LOCAL HISTORY MUSEUMS AND LIBRARIES

Chicago History Museum
1601 North Clark Street
Chicago, Illinois 60614-6071
(312) 642-4600
www.chicagohistory.org
To celebrate its 150th anniversary, the Chicago Historical Society completely renovated its museum space and changed its name to the Chicago History Museum. The new museum, which reopened in September 2006, also features an interactive Children's Gallery. The Web site is also worth visiting for its online exhibits and activities.

Clarke House
1827 South Indiana Avenue
Chicago, Illinois 60616
(312) 326-1480
Take a tour of the Clarke House to see what it was like to be a middle-class family around the time that the city of Chicago came into existence.

Glessner House Museum
1800 South Prairie Avenue
Chicago, IL 60616
(312) 326-1480
www.glessnerhouse.org
Tour the Glessner House and see what life was like for wealthy Chicagoans living at the time of the Haymarket Riots and the World's Columbian Exposition.

Jane Addams Hull-House Museum
800 South Halsted Street
Chicago, IL 60607
(312) 413-5353
http://wall.aa.uic.edu:62730/artifact/
HullHouse.asp
The museum is operated by the University of Illinois-Chicago, and admission is free. Learn about Jane Addams and her efforts to improve the lives of poor Chicagoans.

McCormick Tribune Bridgehouse & Chicago River Museum
376 North Michigan Avenue
Chicago, IL 60610
(312) 977-0227
www.bridgehousemuseum.org
The museum is located within the southwest bridge tower at the corner of Michigan Avenue and the Chicago River. Inside you'll find exhibits and artifacts related to the history of the Chicago River.

Newberry Library
60 West Walton Street
Chicago, IL 60610
(312) 943-9090
www.newberry.org
In addition to all of the research materials on site, the Newberry Library offers seminars in subjects like genealogy and local history. The Newberry also presents exhibits related to their collections, which are especially strong in maps and Native American history.

LOCAL ETHNIC MUSEUMS

Chinese-American Museum of Chicago
238 West 23rd Street
Chicago, IL 606
(312) 949-1000
www.ccamuseum.org
Located in Chinatown, this museum explores the Chinese American experience in Chicago through exhibits, lectures, and research.

Du Sable Museum of African American History
740 East 56th Place
Chicago, IL 60637
(773) 947-0600
www.dusablemuseum.org
The oldest museum of its type in the United States, the DuSable Museum presents exhibits and programs related to the African American experience in Chicago and throughout the United States.

Hellenic Museum and Cultural Center
801 West Adams Avenue, 4th Floor
Chicago, IL 60607
(312) 655-1234
www.hellenicmuseum.org
The Immigrant Gallery re-creates the experiences of Greek immigrants moving to Chicago and other parts of the United States.

Irish American Heritage Center
4626 North Knox Avenue
Chicago, IL 60630
(773) 282-7035
www.irishamhc.com
The museum chronicles the history of Irish peoples from the sixth century on. Exhibits include artifacts from Chicago.

National Museum of Mexican Art
1852 West 19th Street
Chicago, IL 60608
(312) 738-1503
www.nationalmuseumofmexicanart.org
A major part of the museum's ongoing exhibition, *Mexicanidad: Our Past Is Present*, is called "Mexicans Chicago: Huellas Fotograficas." Photographs document 100 years of Mexican history in Chicago.

The Polish Museum of America
984 North Milwaukee Avenue
Chicago, IL 60622
(773) 384-3352
http://pma.prcua.org
Exhibits and photographs show the early history of Polish immigrants to America and Chicago.

Spertus Institute of Jewish Studies
618 South Michigan Avenue
Chicago, IL 60605
(312) 322-1700
www.spertus.edu/index.php
The Spertus Institute was closed for renovations when this book went to print, but the new facility is scheduled to include a Children's Center. Historically, the museum has produced exhibits related to the Jewish experience in general, with some exhibits focusing on Jewish Americans living in Chicago.

Swedish American Museum Center
5211 North Clark Street
Chicago, IL 60640
(773) 728-8111
www.samac.org/index1.html
At this Andersonville museum you can re-create the journey to America made by early Swedish immigrants, play dress-up in traditional Swedish clothing, and make holiday arts and crafts.

ARCHITECTURAL TOURS

Chicago Architecture Foundation
224 South Michigan Avenue
Chicago, Illinois 60604
(312) 922-3432
www.architecture.org
The CAF offers guided tours of Chicago, including its popular Chicago River architecture cruise. Teachers can also call to arrange special tours and presentations for their students.

Frank Lloyd Wright Preservation Trust
(708) 848-1976
www.wrightplus.org
The Trust runs tours of the Frank Lloyd Wright Home and Studio in Oak Park, as well as the Robie House in Chicago's Hyde Park neighborhood.

LOCAL CULTURAL INSTITUTIONS

Art Institute of Chicago
111 South Michigan Avenue
Chicago, IL 60603
(312) 443-3600
www.artic.edu
This world-class art museum of course owns many of the world's most priceless pieces of art. It also has architectural treasures, like the trading room of the Chicago Stock Exchange, and fragments from notable structures designed by Louis Sullivan, Daniel H. Burnham, and Frank Lloyd Wright. The Kraft Education Center at the Art Institute offers activities and resources for kids and their families.

Chicago Children's Museum
700 East Grand Avenue
Chicago, IL 60611
(312) 527-1000
www.chichildrensmuseum.org
This interactive museum on Chicago's Navy Pier is a popular attraction for locals as well as tourists. Kids can climb the rope ladder, build unique structures in "Under Construction," and learn about the physics of water in "WaterWays."

The Field Museum
1400 South Lake Shore Drive
Chicago, IL 60605
(312) 922-9410
www.fieldmuseum.org
This is more than the house of Sue, the famous *T. rex*. You can learn a lot about the geology, archaeology, and anthropology of Chicago at the Field Museum. It also houses approximately 50,000 artifacts collected for the 1893 World's Columbian Exposition. Although many of these artifacts are in storage, the museum is working on digitizing them for online viewing.

Museum of Broadcast Communications
400 North State Street
Chicago, IL 60610
(312) 245-8200
www.museum.tv/home.php
The museum was closed for renovation when this book went to press. The new state-of-the-art facility is scheduled to open sometime in 2007. The museum's collection includes historic television footage, radio program recordings, and print memorabilia. Explore Chicago's role in early radio programs, as well as children's television programming.

Museum of Science and Industry
57th Street and Lake Shore Drive
Chicago, IL 60637
(773) 684-1414
www.msichicago.org
In addition to its many scientific exhibits, this museum has a scale model of downtown Chicago. You can also "take a ride" on the Pioneer Zephyr, a high-speed diesel locomotive which transported travelers from Chicago to various cities in the western United States from 1934 to 1960.

DOWNSTATE DESTINATIONS

Cahokia Mounds Visitor Center
30 Ramey Street
Collinsville, IL 62234
(618) 346-5160
www.cahokiamounds.com
Visit the interpretive center for exhibits showing what life in Cahokia might have been like a thousand years ago, and take a walking tour of the grounds.

The Center for American Archaeology
P.O. Box 366
Kampsville, Illinois 62053
(618) 653-4316
www.caa-archeology.org
Kids can roll up their sleeves and work at archaeological digs during summer programs or field trips. The CAA also offers workshops where you can learn the art of flintknapping.

Dickson Mounds Museum
10956 North Dickson Mounds Road
Lewistown, IL 61542
(309) 547-3721
www.museum.state.il.us/ismsites/dickson
Learn about the Native Americans who inhabited the Illinois River valley as long as 12,000 years ago.

HELPFUL WEB SITES

Chicago Metro History Education Center
www.chicagohistoryfair.org
Learn all about the Chicago History Fair. This site includes schedules, guidelines, and forms needed to compete in the annual history fair. You'll also find tips on selecting a topic and examples of past history fair projects.

Chicago Public Library Digital Collections
www.chipublib.org/digital/digital.html
Includes interactive features on eight topics, including "Chicago's Front Door: The Lakefront," "Remembering Harold: Photographs from the Harold Washington Archives," and "Then and Now: Historic Photographs of Ravenswood and Lake View."

City of Chicago Landmarks
www.cityofchicago.org/Landmarks/Index.html
This Web site contains tours, maps, lists, photographs, and databases, as well as biographies of notable Chicago architects.

The Electronic Encyclopedia of Chicago
www.encyclopedia.chicagohistory.org
The complete contents of *The Encyclopedia of Chicago* are available online.

Graveyards of Chicago
www.graveyards.com/index2.html
An online tour of Chicago's historic graveyards, including Rosehill, Graceland, and Bohemian National.

INDEX